TOFINO GUIDE

John Platenius

Copyright © 2011 Wild Cedar Publishing
All rights reserved.

c/o Tofino Internet Services Ltd.
PO Box 83
Tofino, BC V0R 2Z0
tofino.guide@gmail.com
www.tofino-bc.com

Library and Archives Canada Cataloguing in Publication
Platenius, John, 1974-
    Tofino guide / John Platenius.
ISBN 978-0-9868051-0-3
LCCN 2010907983

    1. Tofino Region (B.C.)--Guidebooks. 2. Pacific Rim National Park Reserve (B.C.)--Guidebooks. 3. Clayoquot Sound Region (B.C.)--Guidebooks.
I. Title.
FC3849.T65A3 2011   917.11'2   C2010-907801-2

Cover Photo
http://tofinophotography.wordpress.com

Interior Photos	pages
Jeff Mikus:	3, 7, 9, 23, 38, 47, 54, 67, 72, 91, 99, 108, 122, 131, 139, 151, 164, 174, 184, 200, 206, 221, 225, 239
James Hudnall:	42, 48, 84, 166, 246, 254
JeremyKoreski.com:	0, 14, 30, 74, 100, 218
Sarah Platenius:	58, 190, 211, 217, 240
Mike Anderson:	118, 152
John Platenius:	29, 115
Michael Farrow:	202
Jay Feaver:	viii
Raphael Glacet:	24

TABLE OF CONTENTS

Introduction . . . . *ix*
    About this Guide x
    Contact Tofino Guide. xi
    Tofino's Top Ten List xii

1: Need to Know Information 1
    Emergency Services 2
    Cyberspace in Tofino 4
    Parking in Tofino. 6
    The Importance of Tide Charts 8
    A Friendly Note to Dog Owners 10
    Rogue Waves 11

2: Getting Here: Routes and Transportation Services 15
    Driving: Ferries to Vancouver Island 16
    Driving: The Route to Tofino 18
    Bus Service to Tofino 20
    Car Rental 21
    Flying. 21

3: Visitor Information Services 25
    The Pacific Rim Visitor Centre at The Junction 26
    The Tofino Visitor Centres. 27

4: Regional Information 31
    Tofino History. 32
    District of Tofino 36
    Nuu-chah-nulth First Nations History and Geography 37
    The UNESCO Clayoquot Sound Biosphere 40
    Meares Island 41
    Culturally Modified Trees (CMT) 43
    Nurse Logs 44
    Top 10 Must-See Trees of Clayoquot Sound 45

5: Tofino's Temperate Climate 49
We get a lot of drizzle here, but when it rains it pours. 50
Tofino Climate Normals: 1971 - 2000 52
Coastal Temperate Rainforest 53
Storm Watching 55
20 Things to Do When it Rains. 56

6: Tofino's Beaches 59
Beachcombing 60
Can we build a campfire on the beach?. 61
Tonquin Beach. 62
MacKenzie Beach 64
Chesterman Beach and Frank Island 66
Cox Bay. 68
Top 10 Beaches of Clayoquot Sound. 70

7: Pacific Rim National Park Reserve. 75
About Pacific Rim National Park Reserve. 76
Fees at Pacific Rim National Park Reserve 76
Wickaninnish Interpretive Centre. 79
Green Point Theatre. 80
Wheelchair Accessibility in Pacific Rim
    National Park Reserve 81
Top 10 Activities in the Pacific Rim National Park Reserve . . . 82

8: Charters & Tours. 85
Whale Watching 86
Bear Watching 89
Hot Springs Tours 90
Birdwatching 92
Cultural Tours 94
Scenic Boat Charters 94
Scenic Flights 95
Sea Kayaking 96
Sport Fishing 97
SCUBA Diving. 99

9: Surfing 101
The Surfing Capital of Canada 102
Where Do I Start? 102

Chesterman Beach Surfing 103
Cox Bay Surfing 104
Long Beach Surfing 105
Surf Shops and Surfing Gear Rentals 106
Surfing Lessons 107

10: Maps 109
Getting Here 110
Pacific Rim National Park Reserve (showing hikes) 112
District of Tofino (showing beaches) 114
Downtown Tofino 116

11: Hiking in Pacific Rim National Park Reserve 119
Don't make us rescue you – Hiking Safety Tips 120
Encounters with Bears, Cougars or Wolves 121
Radar Beaches 123
Radar Hill View Point 125
Bomber Trail 126
Schooner Cove Trail 128
Long Beach 130
Spruce Fringe Trail 132
Combers Beach 133
Rain Forest Trail, Loops A & B 135
Florencia Bay Beach (also called Wreck Bay) 138
Shorepine Bog Trail 140
South Beach Trail 142
Nuu-chah-nulth Trail 144
Gold Mine Trail 146
Willowbrae Trail 149
Half Moon Bay Trail 150

12: Getting off the Peninsula: Wilderness Exploration 153
Self-Guided Sea Kayaking Expeditions 156
Wildside Heritage Trail (on Flores Island) 156
Ahous Bay Trail (on Vargas Island) 159
Big Tree Trail (on Meares Island) 162
Lone Cone Trail (on Meares Island) 165

13: Food, Drink and Dining Out 167
Take-out and Casual Eateries 168
Pubs and Lounges 175
Finer Dining 176
Beer, Wine and Liquor Sales 182
Catering 182
Seafood Stores 183
Foraging for Tofino's Seafood 185
Purchasing a Fishing License (Yes, you need
    this for shellfish, too!). 185
Check for Red Tide before Harvesting Shellfish 186
Can I eat the Mussels? 187
Where can I find Clams in Clayoquot Sound? 187
Finding Oysters in Clayoquot Sound 188
What about live Crabs?. 188

14: Shopping 191
Gifts and Souvenirs 192
Clothing and Outdoor Gear 193
Galleries and Studios 197
Groceries and Snacks 199
Bookstores. 201
Public Market 201

15: Fitness & Leisure 203
Spas, Yoga, Body & Hair Care 204
Gardens: Private and Public 207
Running and Jogging 210
Multi-Use Path (MUP) 211
Bicycle Rentals & Services 212
Salt Water Swimming 212
Fresh Water Swimming 213
Indoor Pools 213
Skatepark, Tennis, Basketball 214
Golfing and Mini Golf 214
Kite Flying and Kiteboarding 215
Rock Climbing 216
Top 10 things to do in Tofino with the Kids 216

16: Accommodation Listings 219
Reservations and Rates 220
Beachfront Resorts, Lodges and Hotels 222
Hotels, Motels, and Resorts (not on the beach) 226
Bed and Breakfasts & Vacation Rentals 230
Hostels 236
Accommodation at Hot Springs Cove 236
Campgrounds 237
Glamping: Glamorous Camping. 238

17: Local Transportation. 241
Tofino Transit 242
The Beach Bus 242
Taxi 242
Water Taxis 242
Boat Launches 244

18: Services. 247
Banking, Foreign Currency Exchange, and ATMs
  (Cash Machines). 248
Fuel Service 248
Laundry & Showers. 249
Pharmacy 249
Library, Museums, Societies 250
Churches. 252
Recycling 252
Tofino Radio 252
Periodicals 253
Post Office 253

19: Recommended Reading. 255

INTRODUCTION

About this Guide

Contact Information

Tofino's Top Ten List

TOFINO GUIDE

ABOUT THIS GUIDE

Tofino Guide has been providing helpful information to our region's visitors for over ten years. In this updated and expanded edition, ***Tofino Guide*** aims to provide detailed and reliable information of all kinds about Tofino, its amenities and its surroundings. In describing the services available in the area, our approach is to be broadly inclusive rather than selectively judgmental. We do our best to present our information in a fair and unbiased manner. We hope we have succeeded and we welcome your comments.

UP TO DATE WITH *TOFINO GUIDE*!

While doing our utmost to keep this print edition of *Tofino Guide* up to date, we recommend that readers also check out our website (www.tofino-bc.com) for the very latest information about and/or changes in local services and businesses. The website is updated continually with hot-off-the-press Tofino news.

Tofino Guide **cannot reply to individual requests for tourist advice or vacancy information. For all such inquiries please contact Tourism Tofino directly:**

Tourism Tofino
PO Box 1140
Tofino, BC V0R 2Z0
Canada
Phone: 250-725-3414
Web: www.tourismtofino.com
Email: info@tourismtofino.com

CONTACT TOFINO GUIDE

We welcome your comments, corrections and suggestions.

Please send all correspondence by email or by mail to the *Tofino Guide* address:

Tofino Guide
c/o Tofino Internet Services Ltd.
PO Box 83
Tofino, BC V0R 2Z0
Canada
Email: tofino.guide@gmail.com
Web: www.tofino-bc.com

TOFINO GUIDE

TOFINO'S TOP TEN LIST

1. Get out on the water! Take a whale watching trip, a shore-cruising boat charter or a guided kayak trip. Much of Clayoquot Sound is accessible only by water and the view of Esowista Peninsula with Meares Island as a backdrop is stunning. On any boat trip, expect to see Lennard Light, bald eagles, harbour seals, sea lions, sometimes harbour porpoises and, with any luck, either grey or humpback whales. (p. 85)

2. GO TO LONG BEACH. Sixteen kilometres of sand awaits you at Canada's most famous beach. Rain or shine. What are you waiting for? (p. 130)

3. Beachcomb along one of the many beaches near Tofino or in the Pacific Rim National Park Reserve. Make it a day by planning for a picnic or BBQ filled with West Coast delights: smoked salmon, grilled oysters, local treats from the bakery. Make your mark, however temporary, with a sandcastle. (p. 60)

4. Visit Meares Island and see the 1500 year old western red cedars. Don't even try and hug one of these grand-daddies unless you are travelling with a few dozen companions – scores of arms are needed! While you are there, walk the Big Tree Trail, noting bald eagle nests and culturally modified trees (p. 162). In addition to the fun on the trail, you will get a short ride across the inlet in a water taxi or in a sea kayak as a bonus adventure (p. 96).

5. Take a day long guided kayaking trip (or if you're experienced just rent a kayak). Getting out in the Sound in a kayak allows you to view marine life up close, and to feel part of this amazing seascape. Curious harbour seals pop their heads out of the water, black bears appear on beaches looking for food, salmon swim beneath you. You can paddle close to double-crested cormorants, great blue herons, and under the stern gaze of bald eagles. Pause often to feel the gentle swell of the ocean passing beneath you. Gliding over beds of kelp, gaze into the water to see purple and orange seastars, delicate jellyfish, and many varieties of seaweed. Listen to the silence. (p. 96)

6. Witness a winter storm from one of the beaches. Between November and February, Tofino will be hit with winds exceeding

80 km per hour, 10 metre swells, and unrelenting horizontal rain. **GO OUTSIDE IN THIS, YOU ASK?** Yes! Get out there and enjoy the show! It is far more exhilarating than watching from indoors. The experience is unforgettable, and you might find you have a beach entirely to yourself. BUT STAY SAFE. Never go close to the immense waves, they are dangerously unpredictable and occasionally an extra large one comes thundering in. (p. 55)

7. Take a day trip to Hot Springs Cove. The trip up and back allows for whale watching, bald eagle spotting and when you get there you can enjoy the pools of hot natural spring water that descend to the ocean below. (p. 90)

8. Enjoy some local wild seafood even if you don't catch it yourself. For bonus points, see how many ways you can discover to eat salmon when you are here. Start with the standard six: grilled, baked, hot smoked, cold smoked, jerked, and poached. Don't forget to try Dungeness crab, freshly shucked oysters, side striped jumbo shrimp, smoked cod, halibut and chips, local snapper and steamed mussels or clams. The seafood platter for two is a standard item in many local restaurants – highly recommended for a broad sampling and stretched tummies. (p. 183)

9. Hike at least one of the trails in the Pacific Rim National Park Reserve. Any one of these trails offers a superb outing. Some of the most interesting trails stay within one type of habitat, such as the Shorepine Bog Trail (wheelchair accessible), Spruce Fringe Trail, and either of the Rain Forest Trail loops. Study the interpretive signs, and after your walk identify the following trees before your vacation is over: western red cedar, Sitka spruce, western hemlock, Douglas fir. (p. 119)

10. Go Surfing. Get instruction from one of the great local surf schools or just rent a surfboard and a wetsuit (yes, you need a wetsuit) and jump in. Tofino is officially the Surfing Capital of Canada and there is almost always a safe beach for first time surfers. Ask the surf school or surf shop where the best beach to learn is given the current conditions, and get ready to have fun. (p. 101)

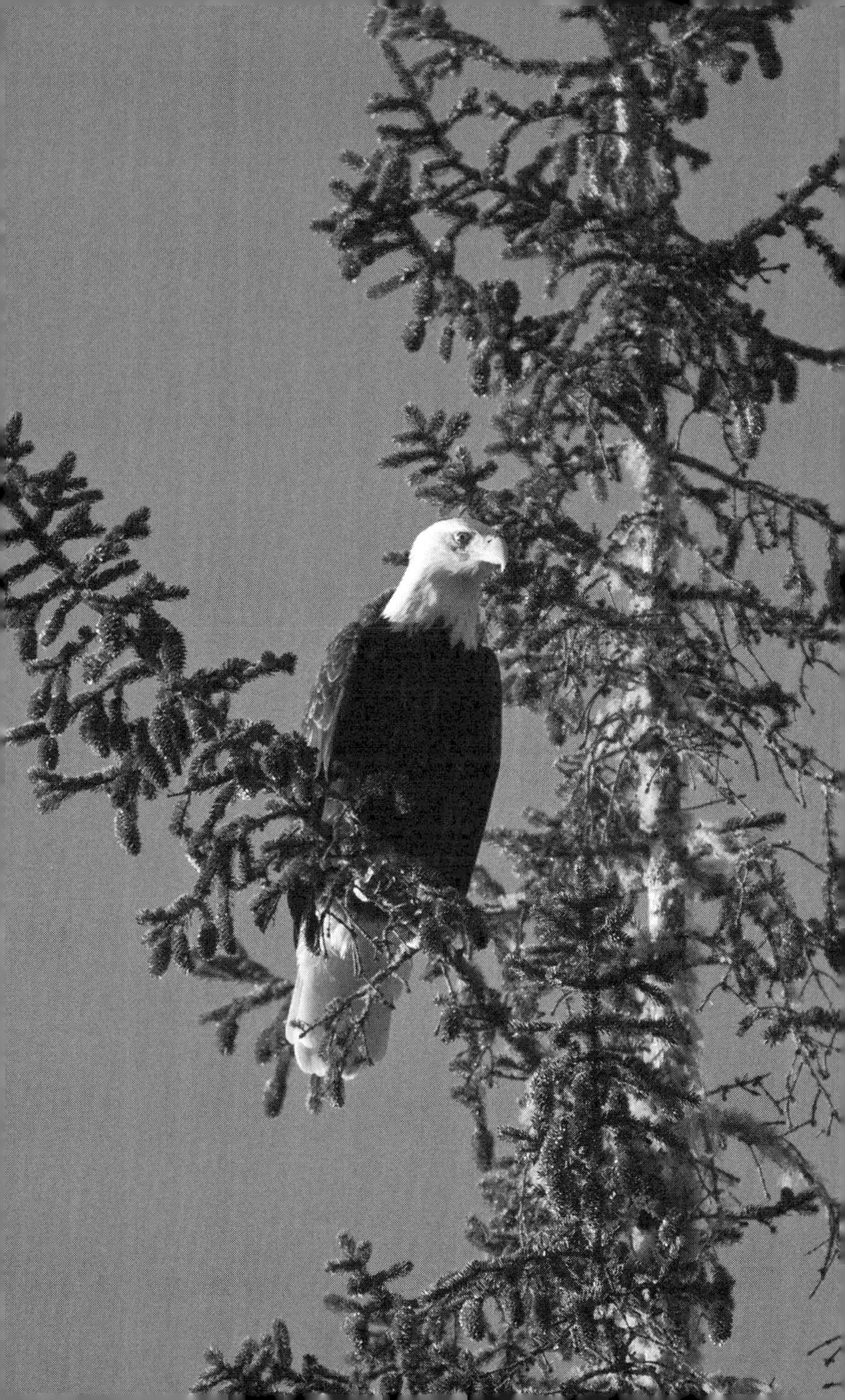

NEED TO KNOW INFORMATION

Emergency Services

Cyberspace in Tofino

Parking in Tofino

The Importance of Tide Charts

A Friendly Note to Dog Owners

Rogue Waves

TOFINO GUIDE

EMERGENCY SERVICES

In any emergency, dial 911 on your telephone.

Tofino General Hospital
261 Neill Street, 250-725-3212; Open 24 Hours daily

Tonquin Medical Clinic
220 First Street, 250-725-3282
For non-emergencies, preferably by appointment. Open: 10 am to 6 pm, Monday to Friday, closes at lunch.

Tofino Dental, Dr. Jameson
First and Neill Street, 250-725-2580
Located below **SOBO**. Open by appointment

**Police Department: RCMP
(Royal Canadian Mounted Police)**
400 Campbell Street, 250-725-3242; Emergencies, call 911

Tofino Coast Guard
322 Main Street, 250-725-3231
VHF Radio Channel 16 (Emergencies, Search and Rescue)

Veterinarian Jane Hunt
Located about 40 km south of Tofino in Port Albion (near Ucluelet) 250-726-2682; Phone for directions and availability

Long Beach Automotive
671 Industrial Way, 250-725-2030
Honest auto repair. Tell the folks at the shop if it is an emergency and they will do their best to get you going. Open Monday-Friday, 8 am – 5 pm

Wet Coast Towing
250-726-8112
(That's **not** a typo...WET Coast Towing) towing, auto lock-outs, flats

DIRECTIONS AND MEASUREMENTS

All distances in this book are given in millimetres (mm), metres (m) or kilometres (km). One **millimetre** equals 0.04 inches. One **metre** equals 1.09 yards. One **kilometre** equals 0.62 miles.

Most distances to or from Tofino are measured from the Tofino Post Office (Canada Post). The Post Office stands at the corner of First and Campbell Streets, the busiest intersection of the town, marked by our only traffic light.

Area measurements are given in hectares. One **hectare** equals 2.47 acres.

Where possible, we indicate direction (north, south, east, west) with a corresponding left/right orientation. When referring to beaches, we give left/right orientation as if you are facing the ocean.

TOFINO GUIDE

CYBERSPACE IN TOFINO

Wireless internet, GPS, and cellular communication all work quite well in and around Tofino. There are, however, a few exceptions:

- There is no cellular phone reception *en route* to Tofino along most of Highway 4 north of Port Alberni. Reception is lost about 10 km north of Port Alberni near Sproat Lake and remains unavailable for about 80 km, beginning again at The Pacific Rim Visitor Centre at The Junction (p. 26).

- Cellular phone reception can be poor in some areas of the Pacific Rim National Park.

- Boaters can rely on cellular communication within roughly 4 km of Tofino; signal strength diminishes from there but remains patchy in some places further than 4 km.

- **GPS reception can be unreliable in the dense temperate rainforest**. If you are planning on relying on GPS for navigation, you should continually check your reception in heavily forested areas.

- Your accommodation provider will likely provide you with **high speed wireless internet** but it is best to ask in advance, if you depend on internet access.

- Wireless internet connections are available throughout most of the commercial section of Tofino between Fourth and First Streets. **Seaview Communications** (www.seaviewcable.net, 250-725-3222) has many wireless hotspots that are available throughout town for a fee and almost every coffee shop and restaurant has a wireless connection in exchange for patronage or for an hourly fee.

- If you left your computer at home you can rent time at the following locations:

  - **Caffe Vincente** (441 Campbell Street, 250-725-2599)
  - **Long Beach Golf Course Pro Shop** (1850 Pacific Rim Highway, 250-725-3332, www.longbeachgolfcourse.com)
  - **Tofino Pharmacy** (360 Campbell Street, 250-725-3101)
  - **Tofino Public Library** (331 Main Street, 250-725-3713)
  - **Tofitian Internet Café** (1180 Pacific Rim Highway, www.tofitian.com)
  - **Tuff Beans** (461 Campbell Street, 250-725-4246, www.tuffbeans.com

TOFINO GUIDE

PARKING IN TOFINO

Most short term vehicle parking in Tofino is free. In the downtown area, many signs indicate where parking is allowed and the time period for which you can park.

Designated short term RV parking is free along the north side of Third Street, in between Campbell and Neill Street. RVs can also hunt down short term parking along First Street, in between Neill Street and Arnet Road.

Long term parking is available for a fee in a large gravel parking area located off Main Street at Third. Buy your pass at the District of Tofino office (p. 36).

Parking at the District of Tofino's beaches is free. This includes the beaches at Tonquin, MacKenzie, Chesterman (North, Middle, South), and Cox Bay. Some beach parking lots fill up on sunny summer days. If all three Chesterman Beach (p. 66) parking lots are full, park alongside Lynn Road or Chesterman Road, making sure your wheels are completely off the pavement. If the two Cox Bay (p. 68) parking lots are full, park at the Cox Bay Visitor Centre (p. 27).

The District of Tofino has **bylaw enforcement officers** and they do **issue tickets for parking infractions**.

PLEASE NOTE THAT parking within the Pacific Rim National Park Reserve requires a Park Pass (p. 76). This includes parking at Long Beach.

PRONOUNCING CLAYOQUOT

You may hear the word Clayoquot pronounced in several ways. In order of those most commonly heard around town, we suggest one of the following:

Cla – kwot

Cla – kwit

Clay – kwot

Take your pick, but whatever you do, never pronounce this word with three syllables, as in Clay – oh – kwat!

Need to Know

THE IMPORTANCE OF TIDE CHARTS

Understanding the ocean's tide cycles during your visit will make your trip safer and more fulfilling. Put simply, the ocean is affected by the combined gravitational effects of the moon, the sun and the rotating earth. In most areas of the world, including ours, there are two high tides and two low tides roughly every 24 hours. When the moon and the sun are aligned, as in a full moon or new moon, the water level in our region can change as much as 4 metres (13 feet) in depth in as little as 6 hours.

Some areas, like Rosie Bay (p. 66) are only accessible at a low tide and access to these regions can rapidly be cut off by rising water. If you are planning on doing any hiking along the shoreline, like the Radar Beaches (p. 123), then **you must know when it is a *flood tide* (rising water) and when it is an *ebb tide* (falling water)**. If you are planning on doing any boating in Clayoquot Sound, make sure to have a solid understanding of the daily tide cycles and bring along your tide chart.

There are two good tide charts that have the full year's tide predictions. The Pacific Rim National Park Reserve publishes a small, free pocket tide calendar that you can pick up at any of the Visitor Centres (p. 25), the Green Point Campground's entry kiosk (p. 237) or the Wickaninnish Interpretive Centre (p. 79). The federal government sells a detailed and more technical tide and current prediction guide that you can purchase for about $10 at the Co-op Hardware Store (p. 194) or Method Marine (p. 249).

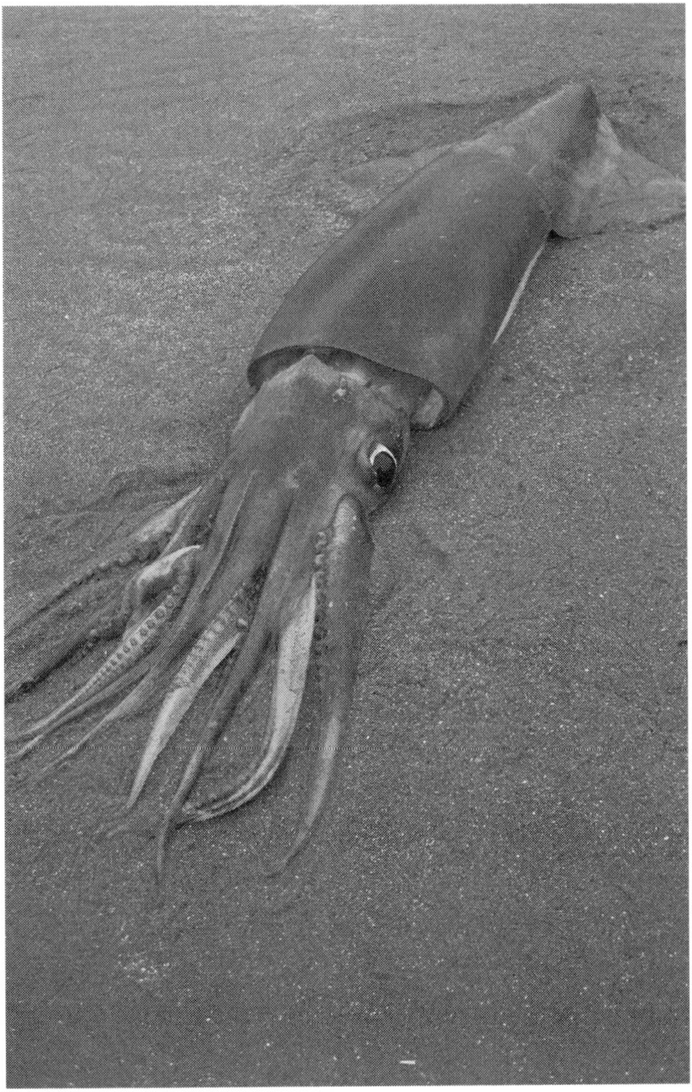

A FRIENDLY NOTE TO DOG OWNERS:

We understand that many visitors travel with dogs. Please remember that because most of the Tofino area is close to or part of a wilderness area, it is important to keep pets leashed when they are outside. Remember that **wandering dogs appeal to cougars as easy targets**.

The District of Tofino has a dogs-on-leash bylaw, and leashes are required in the Pacific Rim National Park Reserve. It is especially important to keep your dog on a leash during the shorebird migration in late April and early May. These birds travel the entire west coast of North America to breed in the north and any energy that they waste can be fatal. A harmless bird chase for Fido could deplete the vital energy reserves of a flock.

Walking dogs on the local beaches is perfectly legal and tons of fun for you and Fido. But wherever you walk your dog, **please bring a bag to pick up your pet's mess**.

ROGUE WAVES

Rogue waves are surges of water that arrive from far off the Pacific coast. They are unpredictable and rise seemingly from nowhere. When they arrive at the shoreline they wash the rocks clean. **Rogue waves are also called killer waves**, and for good reason. In 1997, three visitors to Pacific Rim National Park Reserve were washed off the rocks near **South Beach** (p. 142) and drowned. This occurred when one man in a group of hikers turned his back to the ocean for a moment and was swept into the ocean by a rogue wave. A few panic-filled minutes later, the group spotted his limp body moving in near the shore and attempted to retrieve it. They were swamped by a second wave and two more were killed. You must resist the temptation to get as close to the edge of the water as you can. Stay a safe, smart distance back from the Power of the Pacific. **Never turn your back on the ocean and constantly be aware of the waves**.

TOFINO GUIDE

What to do if you see a...

BLACK BEAR

Relax, it's not a grizzly. Grizzly bears (*Ursus arctos horribilis*) do not live on this part of the coast. If you are in a wilderness area and you spot a black bear (*Ursus americana*), leave it alone and give it lots of room to move. If the bear acts aggressive, stand tall and yell at it. They are nearsighted, so distinguishing your shape at a distance is difficult. But their sense of smell is probably better than any other animal on the planet, beating the bloodhound by far. Most often a bear in the wild that does not seem shy will simply be curious to know what your strong foreign smell is all about.

Bears have been seen walking the sidewalks in downtown Tofino. If you see a black bear in the village, walk away. **Never try to get closer to a bear in order to take pictures. And never ever feed bears**. Once they have tasted human food, bears become habituated to being around civilization. This is dangerous for humans and bears. As the bears become more comfortable in a human environment, they become more aggressive and less shy. If a bear is conditioned to eating human food, it is almost always killed for safety reasons. Through a provincial program called Bear Aware (www.bearaware.bc.ca), Tofino has become increasingly Bear Smart and the number of problem bears has been steadily decreasing.

See page 121 for more information about bear encounters.

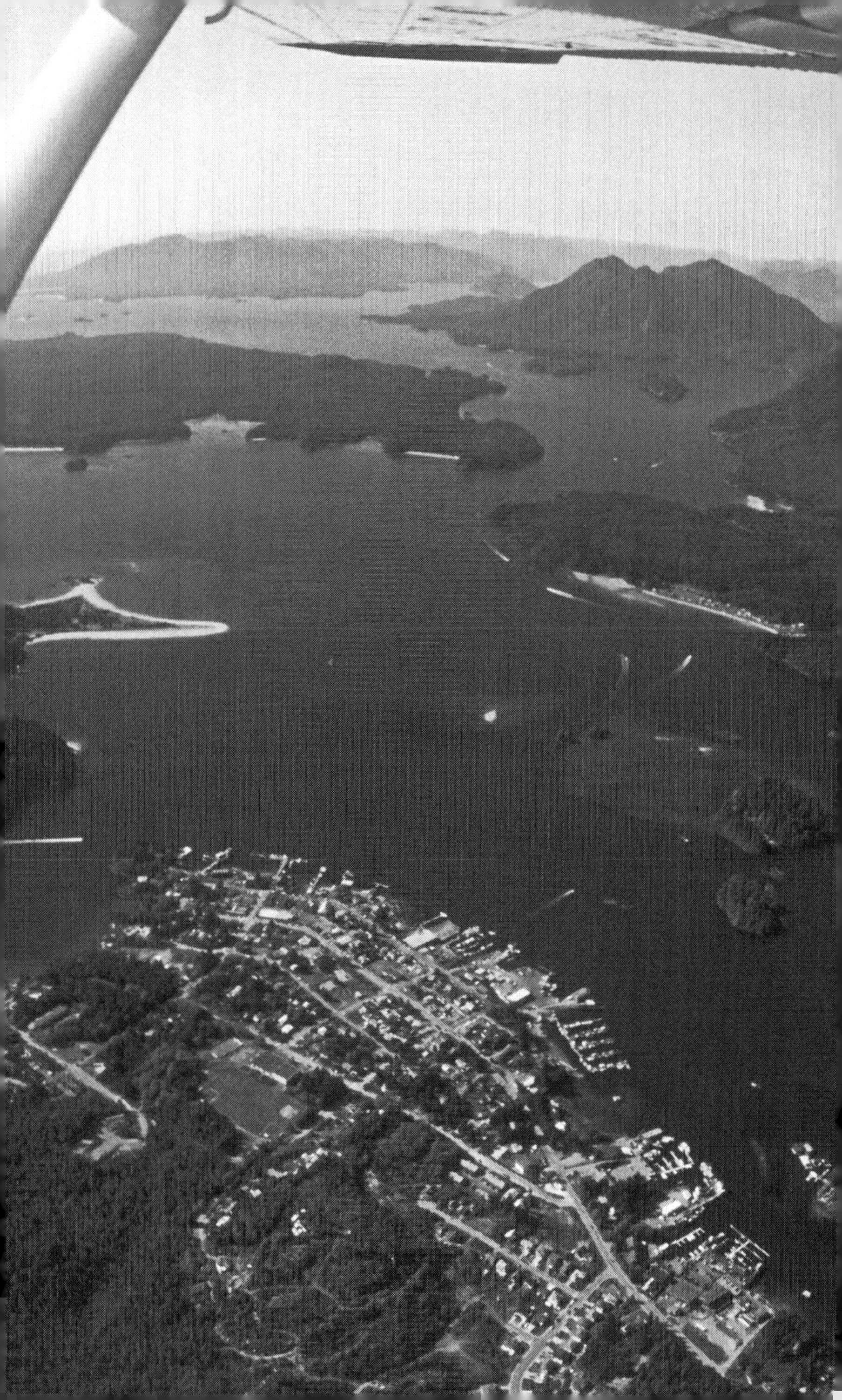

GETTING HERE: ROUTES AND TRANSPORTATION SERVICES

Driving: Ferries to Vancouver Island

Driving: The Route to Tofino

Bus Service to Tofino

Car Rental

Flying

TOFINO GUIDE

DRIVING: GETTING TO VANCOUVER ISLAND

Ferry Information
Tofino is located on Vancouver Island. If you are driving here you have to take a ferry. The most efficient vehicle route from the mainland (with one exception described below) is to take a BC Ferry either from Tsawwassen (about 30 km south of Vancouver) or Horseshoe Bay (about 15 km northwest of Vancouver).

If you are travelling through or from Port Angeles or Olympic National Park, Washington, the most efficient ferry to take is the Black Ball *MV Coho* (Blackball Express) from Port Angeles to Victoria, on the southern tip of Vancouver Island. If you prefer the scenic marine route through the San Juan Islands, you can board a Washington State Ferry in Anacortes, about 40 km south of Bellingham, Washington. See **Other Ferries** below (p. 18) for more information about travelling on the *MV Coho* and the Washington State Ferries.

BC Ferries
888-223-3779, www.bcferries.com
Reliable, scheduled vehicle and passenger ferry service from the mainland to Vancouver Island is provided by BC Ferries.

BC Ferries' Routes, Mainland Vancouver to Vancouver Island:
- Vancouver to Nanaimo (Tsawwassen to Duke Point)
- West Vancouver to Nanaimo (Horseshoe Bay to Departure Bay)
- Vancouver to Victoria (Tsawwassen to Swartz Bay)

There are three ways to get to Vancouver Island from Vancouver with BC Ferries. The best way depends on where you are in Vancouver, and whether or not you wish to visit Victoria on your way to Tofino.

Option #1
If you are travelling direct to Tofino from the Vancouver Airport, Seattle or other places to the south take the Tsawwassen ferry (south of Vancouver) to Duke Point (south of Nanaimo)

Option #2
If you are travelling direct to Tofino from downtown Vancouver or the Trans Canada Highway you have a choice between the Horseshoe Bay (northwest of Vancouver) to Departure Bay (downtown Nanaimo) or Tsawwassen to Duke Point route. If you are travelling between July and August or on a busy long weekend, it may be best to use the Tsawwassen terminal because it is larger and generally has shorter wait times. You can check BC Ferries' website (www.bcferries.com) or phone system (888-223-3779) to see which terminal is less busy. If the terminals are not predicted to be busy, take whichever terminal is closer to you.

Option #3
If you are visiting Victoria on your way to Tofino, take the Tsawwassen ferry (south of Vancouver) to Swartz Bay (north of Victoria).

Ferry reservations are recommended in the summer months and holidays. You must arrive at least 30 minutes before your reservation time. Reservations cost an extra $17 per vehicle. If you are walking on the ferry without a vehicle, reservations are not necessary.

Ferry reservations can be made online (www.bcferries.com) or by phone (888-223-3779). Know your route before attempting to make reservations.

Other Ferry Services
These ferries apply to travellers to or from various locations in Washington State. These ferries have daily scheduled departures year-round, but have fewer daily sailings than BC Ferries. All of the ferries between Vancouver Island and Washington State are smaller than the BC Ferries listed above, making schedules slightly unpredictable in the stormy winter months.

If you are walking on the ferry from Seattle:

Victoria Clipper, 250-382-8100, www.clippervacations.com
- Passenger service only (no vehicles) between downtown Victoria and downtown Seattle
- 2.5 hour crossing

If you are in the Port Angeles area:

M.V. Coho/Blackball Express, 250-386-2202, www.cohoferry.com
- Passenger and vehicle service between downtown Victoria and Port Angeles, Washington
- 1 hour 35 minute crossing

If you are on the San Juan Islands:

Washington State Ferries, 206-464-6400, www.wsdot.wa.gov/ferries
- Passenger and vehicle service between Sidney, BC (north of Victoria) and Anacortes, Washington (just outside Bellingham). **This is a different terminal from the one used by BC Ferries in Swartz Bay, about 3 km north of Sidney.**
- 3 hour crossing

DRIVING: THE ROUTE TO TOFINO

From Victoria, drive north on Highway 1. Officially called the Trans Canada Highway, this is known locally as the Island Highway. After about 1.5 hours and some 100 km, you will be approaching Nanaimo (pronounced Nan-eye-mo). Be on the alert for signs indicating Parksville and Campbell River. **You want to follow these signs**, at least at this point. They will direct you into an exit lane on the right, across an overpass and onto a road bypassing Nanaimo completely. You are now on **Highway 19**. If you miss this turnoff, you will continue straight ahead and into downtown Nanaimo (a fine town, but you don't need to go there en route to Tofino). If you need to stop for supplies, Highway 19 will take you to Woodgrove Centre shopping mall, 18 km north of the turnoff, at Exit #28, Aulds Road.

From the intersection at Aulds Road and Highway 19, drive 31 km and **watch for signs to Port Alberni**. Take Exit #60 off Highway 19 and follow the signs to Port Alberni, 38 km ahead. **You are now on Highway 4**. Consider stopping after 19 km at Cathedral Grove in MacMillan Provincial Park. Here you can follow short hiking trails past giant Douglas fir (*Pseudotsuga menziesii*) and western red cedar (*Thuja plicata*) trees. Toilet facilities are available.

Along the highway through **Port Alberni** you will find many large stores, fast food chains and plenty of gas stations. Turn right at the T-intersection in Port Alberni and follow signs to Ucluelet/Tofino. **Check your fuel level**, because there is only one more gas station (1 km ahead on your right) between here and Tofino, 122 km away.

Now get comfortable and be patient. The drive from Port Alberni to Tofino is not far (122 km), but it is curvy, often steep, and in places dangerous. **If you are driving between the months of November and March be prepared for snow in higher elevations**. This section of the highway is a good area to remember that British Columbia's driving etiquette dictates that **slower vehicles should pull over to the side of the road to let faster vehicles move ahead**. There are a number of lovely pullover areas along the Kennedy River and Kennedy Lake throughout this section of the trip that allow you to get out and explore the water's edge.

After about an hour's drive, you will reach the Pacific Rim Visitor Centre at The Junction (p. 26), stop for information, or simply turn right and drive the remaining 30 km to Tofino. If you decide to stop at one of the Long Beach parking areas to stretch your legs on the beach, make sure to purchase your Park Pass (p. 76), even if you only intend to stop for a few minutes. These parking areas are well monitored and you will likely be fined if you do not purchase your Park Pass.

Driving Times
Victoria to Tofino: About 5 hours including a few stops and a quick bite to eat.

Nanaimo to Tofino: About 3 hours including a few brief stops.
Port Alberni to Tofino: About 2 hours including a brief stop.

BUS SERVICE TO TOFINO

Tofino Bus runs regularly scheduled, daily bus service to Tofino from bus depots in Vancouver, Victoria, Nanaimo and Comox / Courtenay. The bus connects with walk-off passengers on some BC Ferries routes from Horseshoe Bay (northwest Vancouver) to Departure Bay (downtown Nanaimo).

No airport connections are available to Tofino Bus. If you are flying to Vancouver and hoping to ride the bus to Tofino it is best to ride the Sky Train (like a subway, but on rails above ground; 604-953-3333, www.translink.ca) from the airport to Vancouver's downtown bus depot and connect to Tofino.

Tofino Bus
346 Campbell Street, 866-986-3466 or 250-725-2871,
www.tofinobus.com
- Departs daily – check schedules and rates on the website or by phone.
- Tofino Bus and BC Ferries will transport your gear including surfboards and bikes
- Make a reservation through the website or by phone.

CAR RENTAL

Tofino has only one car rental outfit, located at the Tofino Airport. Pick up and drop off service is available with prior arrangement.

Budget Car and Truck Rental
Located at the Tofino Airport (p. 22), 250-725-2060 or 888-368-7368, www.bcbudget.com

FLYING

Travelling to Tofino from Major Airports
If connecting with a flight to the Tofino Airport is not an option, long distance travellers arriving by air have many choices. We have listed the four simplest methods below.

1. Fly to Seattle, rent a car and drive to the Tsawwassen Ferry Terminal (p. 16). Total trip time from Seattle to Tofino should be about 10 hours, depending on the US/Canada border crossing and your ferry connection.
2. Fly to Vancouver International Airport (YVR), rent a car and drive to the Tsawwassen Ferry Terminal (p. 16). Total trip time from the Vancouver International Airport to Tofino should be about 6 hours, depending on your ferry connection.
3. Fly to Vancouver International Airport, connect with a WestJet flight to Comox Valley Airport (YQQ) on Vancouver Island and rent a car. Total driving time from the Comox Valley Airport to Tofino is about 3.5 hours.
4. Fly to Vancouver International Airport, connect with an Air Canada flight to Nanaimo Airport (YCD) on Vancouver Island and rent a car. Total driving time from the Nanaimo Airport is about 3 hours. Be aware that Nanaimo Airport can often be fogged in during the winter, causing cancellations.

If none of the above options fit, try investigating connections at the Victoria International Airport (YYJ).

TOFINO GUIDE

Flying into Tofino Airport (YAZ)
A small terminal services scheduled and chartered flights from Vancouver aboard small jets and twin engine aircraft.

These flights leave Vancouver International Airport's South Terminal, a small distance from the main terminal of Vancouver International Airport. **Orca Air** provides a free shuttle from the main terminal to the South Terminal, and taxi service is also available. Allow at least one hour between flights to ensure a smooth connection.

The **Tofino Airport terminal** is located 17.1 km outside of Tofino down Airport Road, directly across (north) from the Long Beach parking access (p. 130). Drive about a kilometre down Airport Road until you see the obvious airport terminal building where the check-in counter is located.

In the summer months, fog in Tofino commonly delays flights. Orca Air has various contingency plans, depending on weather conditions.

Phone Orca Air for schedules, rates and questions.

Orca Air
Vancouver International Airport (YVR, South Terminal), 888-359-6722, www.flyorcaair.com

Orca Air has **daily scheduled flights between Vancouver and Tofino**. Call or look on their website for schedule and rates.

Local Airlines (Small seaplane service)
In addition to scenic flights, Tofino's two local airlines offer seaplane service to and from Vancouver and other regional destinations. Phone **Atleo Air** or **Tofino Air** for scheduling and pricing details.

Atleo Air
50 Wingen Lane, 866-662-8536 or 250-725-2205,
www.atleoair.com

Tofino Air
50 First Street, 866-486-3247 or 250-725-4454,
www.tofinoair.ca

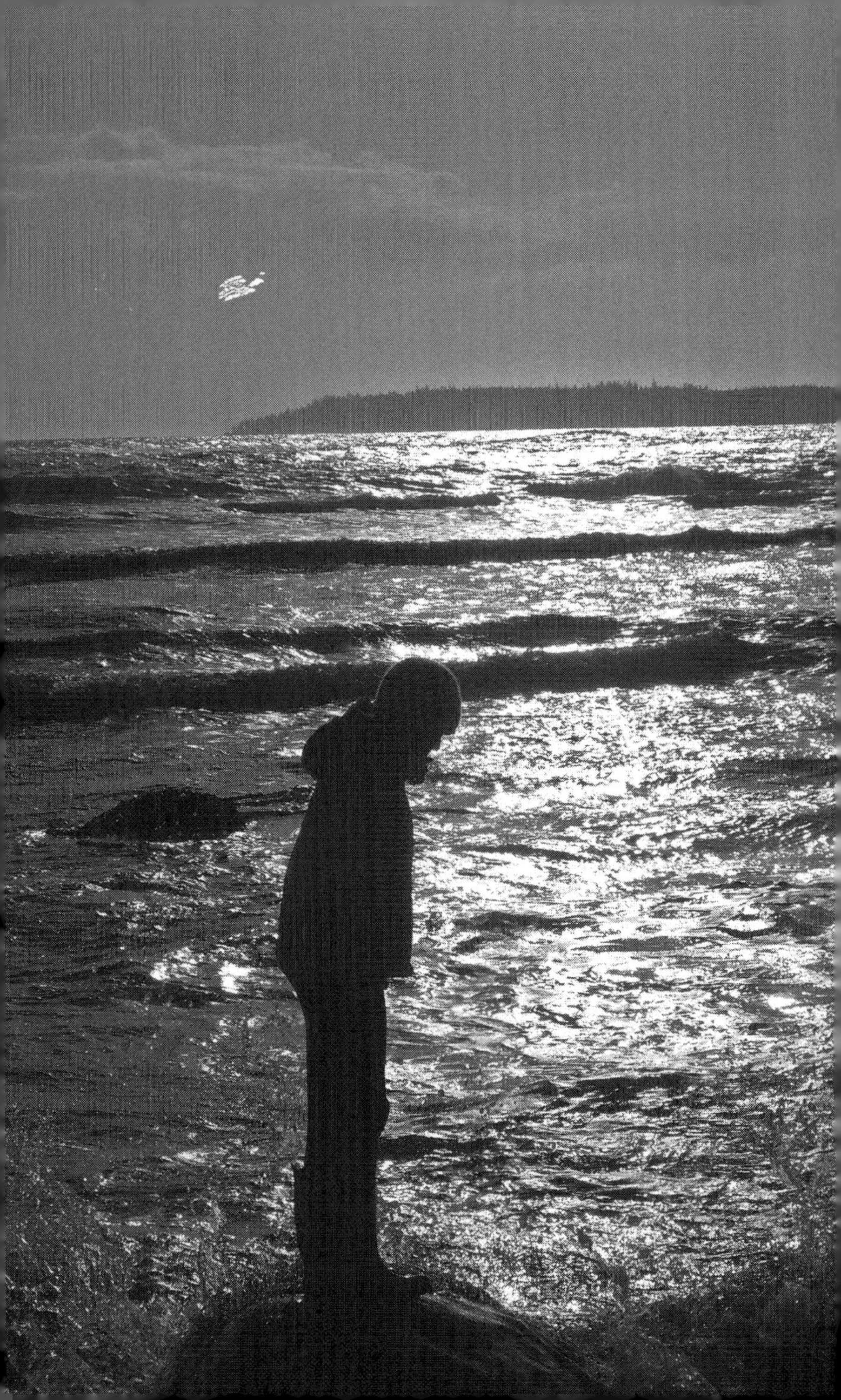

VISITOR INFORMATION SERVICES

The Pacific Rim Visitor Centre at The Junction

The Tofino Visitor Centres

TOFINO GUIDE

THE PACIFIC RIM VISITOR CENTRE AT THE JUNCTION

After driving 92 km from Port Alberni toward Tofino you will arrive at a T-intersection locals call The Junction. On your right you will see the **Pacific Rim Visitor Centre**, an information centre for the villages of Ucluelet and Tofino and for the Pacific Rim National Park Reserve. The folks in the building provide helpful regional advice and can point you to good visual resources to help you prepare you for your vacation. Here you can purchase a Park Pass for the Pacific Rim National Park Reserve. Park Passes are also available at each of the parking areas within the park and at the two Tofino Visitor Centres (p. 27). For more on permits and fees at the Pacific Rim National Park Reserve (p. 76).

Hours of Operation		
Mid October to Mid March	Tuesday - Saturday	10 am - 4 pm
Mid March to July 1	Daily	10 am - 4 pm
July 1 to Early September	Daily	9 am - 7 pm
Early September to Mid-October	Tuesday - Saturday	9 am - 5 pm

250-725-4600
www.pacificrimvisitor.ca

THE TOFINO VISITOR CENTRES

If you are looking for old-fashioned personal advice, and tired of tweets, texts and websites, Tofino's two **Visitor Information Centres** provide excellent support. The separate outposts, one near Cox Bay on the Pacific Rim Highway and one downtown, are up to date with hotel, resort, bed and breakfast or vacation rental vacancies. Vacancies are posted on their website and in their offices on a daily basis. In addition to operating these visitor centres **Tourism Tofino** fields inquiries by phone or email. Both of these Visitor Centres sell Park Passes to the Pacific Rim National Park Reserve (p. 76).

Hours of Operation		
January 2 to Mid May	Daily	10 am - 4 pm
Mid May to Early September	Daily	10 am - 6 pm
Early September to December 23	Tuesday - Saturday	10 am - 4 pm
December 24 to January 1	**Closed**	**Closed**

Cox Bay Visitor Centre
As you drive into town this small building on the right of the highway is one of the first signs that you are – at last – reaching Tofino. Watch for a large **Tourism Tofino** sign just after the Long Beach Lodge Resort and Cox Bay Beach Resort. The official address is 1426 Pacific Rim Highway, but you are best advised to watch for the building, not the address.

Downtown Visitor Centre
Located at 455 Campbell Street, between Fourth and Third streets, the downtown Visitor Centre is in the same building as Mermaid Tales Bookstore and Castaways Second Hand Scores clothing store.

Contact:
www.tourismtofino.com
info@tourismtofino.com
250-725-3414

TOFINO GUIDE

What to do if you see a…

BANANA SLUG

Start counting; you'll probably see lots more. Estimate its size. The Pacific banana slug (*Ariolimax columbianus*) is the second-largest species of terrestrial slug in the world, growing up to 25 centimetres (9.8 in) long. Usually bright yellow they can also be green, brown, or white. Some slugs have black spots.

Admire its shiny trail of slime – without being wrapped in this marvellous mucus, the poor slug would be dehydrated. The slime also contains pheromones to attract other slugs for mating. Slugs are hermaphrodites, and reproduce by exchanging sperm with their mate. They produce up to 75 translucent eggs, which are laid in a log or on leaves. The eggs are abandoned as soon as the clutch is laid, and the slug moves off, slow, slimy and happy in its damp rainforest world. Enjoy watching it stroll away.

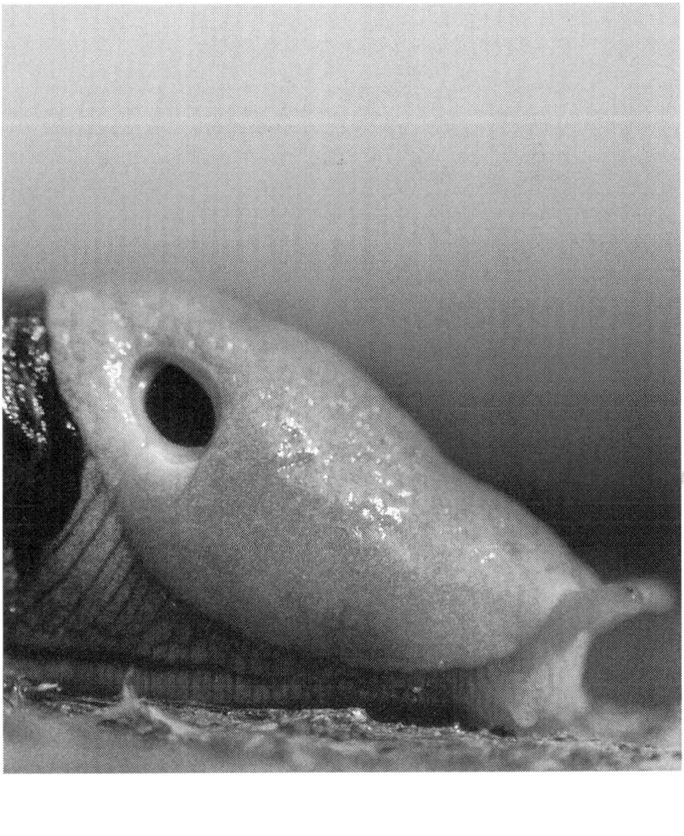

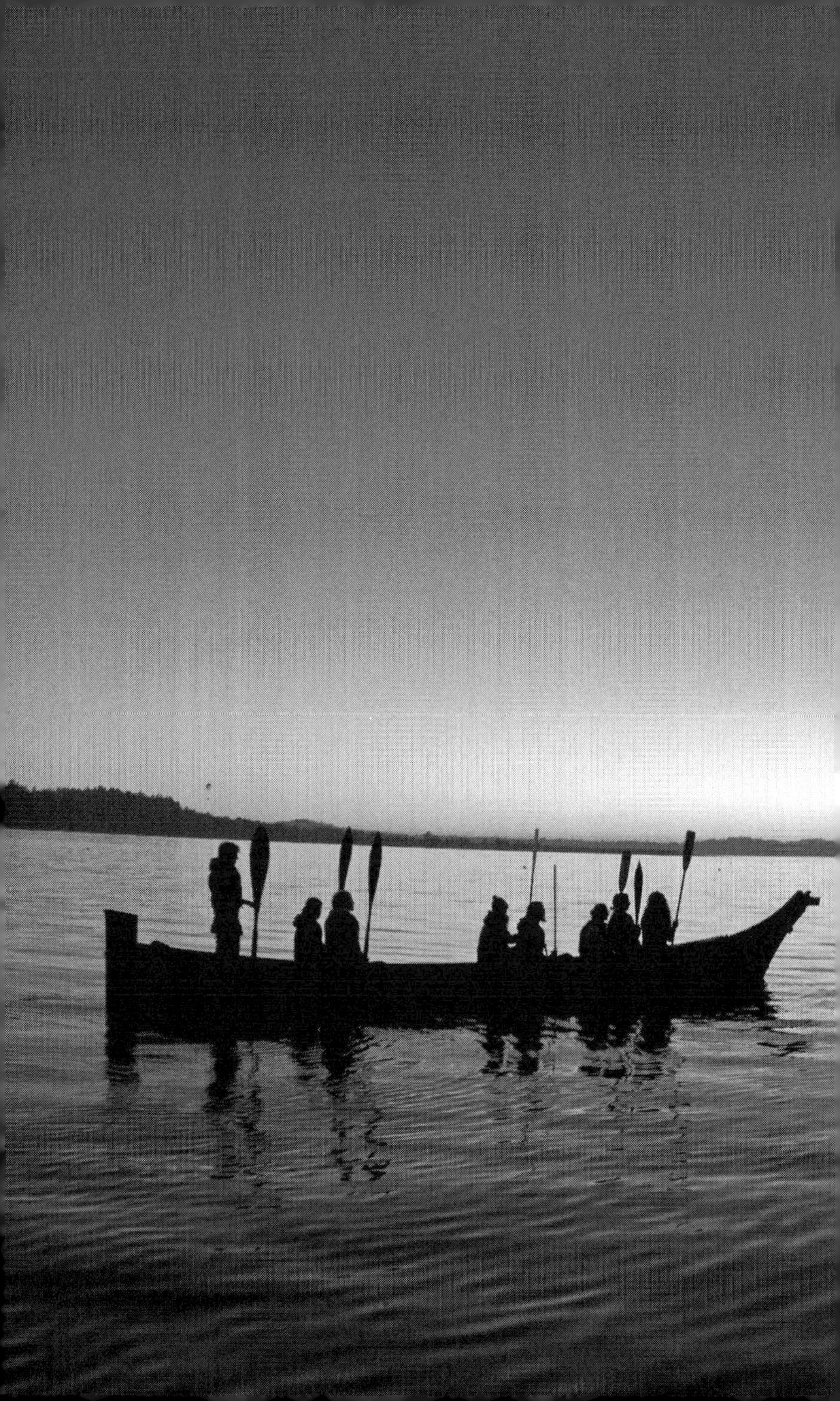

REGIONAL INFORMATION

Tofino History

District of Tofino

*Nuu-chah-nulth First Nations
History and Geography*

The UNESCO Clayoquot Sound Biosphere

Meares Island

Culturally Modified Trees (CMT)

Nurse Logs

Top 10 Must-See Trees of Clayoquot Sound

TOFINO GUIDE

TOFINO HISTORY

Tofino is located in a geographical region called Clayoquot Sound, comprising about 400,000 hectares of land and marine inlets, all draining into a central marine catchment area. The **Nuu-chah-nulth First Nations** (p. 37) have made Clayoquot Sound their home for several thousand years. The Tla-o-qui-aht Village of Opitsaht (across the water from Tofino on Meares Island) is thought to have been continuously inhabited for at least the past 5,000 years, according to carbon dating of a long-buried stash of discarded clamshells. **The word Clayoquot comes from Tla-o-qui-aht**.

The earliest recorded European contact with Vancouver Island's First Nations residents occurred just north of Clayoquot Sound, between Estevan Point and the Escalante River. In 1774 Captain Juan Pérez was sent north by the viceroy of New Spain to reassert the long standing Spanish claim on the west coast of North America. Pérez reached the Queen Charlotte Islands in July, 1774. After some trading with the Haida people from aboard the *Santiago*, Pérez turned south and made contact with Hesquiaht people near what are now called Perez Rocks, approximately 40 km north of Tofino. Curiously, Pérez and his crew did not go ashore.

History buffs will appreciate that Pérez preceded the more celebrated Captain James Cook, who arrived three years later at Nootka Island, in the spring of 1778. Cook claimed the region for Britain, giving rise to heated interactions between the British and the Spanish. War was averted through various agreements outlined in the three Nootka Conventions signed between 1790 and 1794.

During the 1792 exploration of Vancouver Island by Captains Galiano and Valdez, Clayoquot Sound's southernmost inlet gained the name Tofino Inlet. **The name honoured Vincente Tofiño, a Spanish hydrographer** who taught Galiano cartography during the expedition.

The current townsite of Tofino was officially established in 1909 on the Esowista peninsula, taking its name from Tofino Inlet. Until this time, the outpost called Clayoquot was the main European settlement in the area. Located on Stubbs Island, about 1.5 km across the water from the current site of Tofino, Clayoquot had been a fur trading post on and off since the late 1850s. By the turn of the century it boasted a store, post office, hotel, saloon, dock, and a small resident population.

> You can get a good view of the original Clayoquot village site on Stubbs Island from the First Street dock. Standing on the dock, look left (west) to the island with the sandy beach. Stubbs Island is privately owned, but **if you are lucky enough to find yourself in Tofino for the Victoria Day long weekend in the middle of May, the island and its gardens are open for public viewing**. Line up on the First Street dock and hop on board one of the free water taxis that ferry visitors back and forth all afternoon on both Saturday and Sunday.

By the late 1890s, a scattered bunch of homesteads had appeared on the Esowista Peninsula, across the water from Clayoquot. Gradually, the new townsite of Tofino took shape here, as more settlers arrived, mostly Norwegian, Scots, and English. The Anglican Church (still standing at Second Street and Main) was built in 1913 after the Church of England provided funds, instructing that a church be built on the most beautiful spot on Vancouver Island.

The idea of Tofino as a tourist destination has been around for a long time but the reality grew slowly decade by decade. Tourism in the region dates back to the late 1800s when the occasional adventurous traveller would hitch a ride on the steamships transporting miners, fur traders and their equipment up the coast from Victoria. But through the early decades of the 1900s this region was mostly known as an isolated maritime trading town, earning the nickname "Tough City" for its long, rainy and tempestuous winters.

TOFINO GUIDE

In 1959 a long-awaited logging road was punched through the mountains between Port Alberni and the coast. The earliest road travellers, eager to reach the ocean, could only use the logging road on the weekends when loggers had days off. Over time, restrictions on road use eased, and Tofino became an increasingly popular destination. By the late 1960s young people arrived in droves, striking up makeshift camps at a few different beaches in the Long Beach region. At around this time, surfers began to appear on the beaches, at first just a few, the forerunners of today's thriving surf culture. In 1970, Pacific Rim National Park was created. The road was paved in 1972, making it Canada's only paved road to the open Pacific Ocean. Accordingly, Tofino became the official western terminus of the Trans Canada Highway, as evidenced by the official sign at the First Street dock.

In 1993 Tofino and Clayoquot Sound found themselves in the limelight, both nationally and internationally. After a contentious summer in the woods, 856 activists were arrested for protesting the practice of clearcut logging at Kennedy Lake, just south of Tofino. The protest garnered world-wide media attention and stood as the largest mass arrest in Canadian history, until June 2010 when 900 protesters were arrested at the G20 Summit in Toronto.

The recognition of Clayoquot Sound by the United Nations as a **UNESCO Biosphere Reserve** in January 2000 (p. 40) is the region's most recent international distinction, recognizing the area as one of unparalleled natural and cultural riches.

Today, Tofino is Tourism. Clayoquot Sound welcomes between 750,000 and a million visitors annually. These folks migrate here with, and sometimes because of, other returning visitors. Every year in March about 25,000 grey whales pass through Clayoquot Sound en route from Baja to Alaska. Every April and May hundreds of thousands of shorebirds stop to gorge themselves on Clayoquot Sound's nourishing mudflats and sandy beaches before following the whales north. And then there are the salmon. Millions of salmon – five different species in all – mingle and feed in the inshore and offshore waters throughout the summer before the fall rains point them to the rivers and streams where they return to spawn.

Accessible, environmentally rich areas like ours are rare treasures, found in few other locations on the planet. Many residents take preservation of the environment hyper-seriously, evidenced by how local people banded together to save an 800 year old tree in the town centre in 2001. The effort to save this tree, known as the Eik Cedar (pronounced 'ike') attracted significant media attention. See page 45 for more about this tree.

Looking to the future, Tofino's residents and visitors aim to collaborate on projects that will enhance and build upon our vibrant community. And we think big. One of our dreams, scheduled to be completed in 2011, is to build a hiking trail through dense forest and over rocky ocean headlands. This trail will be an extension of the short Tonquin Trail (p. 62), connecting it with the Multi-Use Path (p. 211) near MacKenzie Beach. Another dream, still in the planning phases, is to build the West Coast Recreation Centre, including an Olympic-sized pool and ice skating facility near the airport.

TOFINO GUIDE

DISTRICT OF TOFINO

Throughout this book you will read references to the **District of Tofino**. The term District means that Tofino is one of approximately 160 municipal districts in British Columbia that are incorporated by the province. Tofino, like all of BC's municipal districts, is governed by a Mayor and Council. Services that the District of Tofino oversees include drinking water, sewer, fire protection, garbage/recycling collection, land use planning, parking, building inspection, and municipal parks.

The southern boundary of the District of Tofino abuts onto the northern border of the Pacific Rim National Park Reserve, just south of Cox Bay. The northern border of the District extends a few hundred metres north of the tip of Esowista Peninsula, surrounding a few of the small islands that you can see from the village. The entire District covers 1,060 hectares (about 2,600 acres).

District of Tofino by the Numbers

- Official population: 1,655*

- Estimated population in 2010, including transient workers: About 2000

- Population increase 2001 to 2006: 12.9%*

*2006 Canadian Census data

District of Tofino

121 Third Street at Campbell, 250-725-3229,
www.tofino.ca
Office Hours: Mon to Fri, 9 am to 4 pm

NUU-CHAH-NULTH FIRST NATIONS HISTORY AND GEOGRAPHY

Throughout this guide we use the term **First Nations** when speaking of the aboriginal population. This is generally the preferred term when speaking about Canada's original inhabitants.

Most of the west coast of Vancouver Island is home to the **Nuu-chah-nulth group of First Nations**. The term Nuu-chah-nulth translates as "all along the mountains and sea," according to a Nuu-chah-nulth elder, Nelson Keitlah. The Nuu-chah-nulth people were called **Nootka** from the late 1700s until the mid 1900s. Legend has it that the first explorers heard the local people saying "nootka, nootka" which means "go around, go around." They may have thought that the people were referring to the island where they were living, and applied the name to the people as well. This name survives today with Nootka Island and Nootka Sound, just north of Clayoquot Sound.

The Nuu-chah-nulth territories lie along the west coast of Vancouver Island, between the prominent Brooks Peninsula to the north and Carmanah Point to the south, just north of the village of Port Renfrew. In the Nuu-chah-nulth cultures, their traditional areas are referred to as *ha'houlthee*. These territories are now referred to as Nations. To use the Tofino area as an example, the surrounding land is called the Tla-o-qui-aht Nation, and the local aboriginal people are the Tla-o-qui-aht First Nation.

There are 14 separate Nuu-chah-nulth Nations (see table below). Each Nation is governed through a combination of hereditary and elected chiefs and councils. Of the approximately 8500 registered Nuu-chah-nulth people, about 6000 live within the 14 Nations. The Nuu-chah-nulth people and territories are collectively governed by the Nuu-chah-nulth Tribal Council (NTC). The NTC takes care of different programs and services including fisheries, education, child welfare and health. The NTC also publishes a newspaper called **Ha-Shilth-Sa**, an excellent resource if you would like to learn more about Nuu-chah-nulth politics and current events (www.nuuchahnulth.org/tribal-council/hashilth.html).

FIRST NATIONS CONTACTS IN CLAYOQUOT SOUND:

The traditional territories of the Tla-o-quiaht, Ahousaht and Hesquiaht are located in Clayoquot Sound.

Tla-o-qui-aht First Nation 250-725-3233, www.tla-o-qui-aht.org

Ahoushat First Nation 250-670-9531, www.ahousaht.ca

Hesquiaht First Nation 250-670-1106

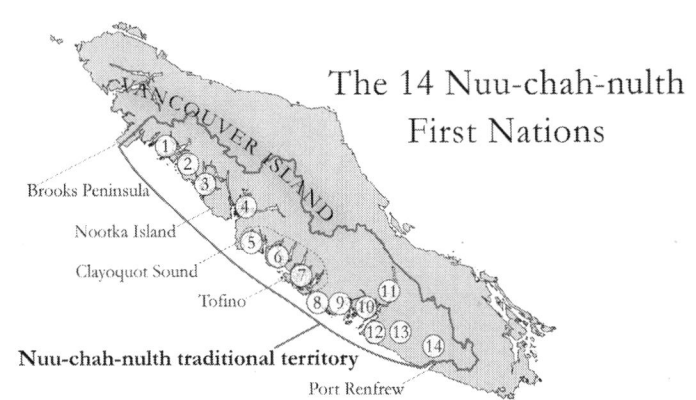

The 14 Nuu-chah-nulth First Nations

Brooks Peninsula
Nootka Island
Clayoquot Sound
Tofino

Nuu-chah-nulth traditional territory

Port Renfrew

Northern Region	Map	Pronunciation*	Population (yr measured)**
Kyuquot/Cheklesahht	1	Ky-you-kut/Check-le-set	498 (2007)
Ehattesaht	2	Eh-hat-eh-sat	331 (2008)
Nuchatlaht	3	Noo-hat-lat	174 (2008)
Mowachat/Muchalaht	4	Mow-a-chat/Much-a-lat	545 (2008)
Central Region			
Hesquiaht	5	Hesh-kwit	661 (2008)
Ahousaht	6	A-house-sat	1,870 (2008)
Tla-o-qui-aht	7	T-lay-quat	945 (2008)
Ucluelet	8	U-clue-let	608 (2007)
Toquaht	9	Toe-kwat	124 (2007)
Southern Region			
Hupacasath	10	Hoop-a-ches-at	257 (2006)
Tse-shaht	11	Tse-shat	969 (2008)
Uchucklesaht	12	U-chuck-le-sat	189 (2007)
Huu-ay-aht	13	Oo-hi-at	623 (2007)
Ditidaht	14	Dit-ee-dat	683 (2006)

*Pronunciations from the *Pronunciation Guide to First Nations in British Columbia, BC Stats*

**Population statistics from the *Ministry of Aboriginal Relations and Reconciliation: Registered Indian Population by Sex and Residence, Indian and Northern Affairs*. Note that population is a measure of band members, not population in a village. For example, the population of Marktosis, the Ahousaht village, is about 900, but the number of registered band members is 1,870.

TOFINO GUIDE

THE UNESCO CLAYOQUOT SOUND BIOSPHERE

On January 21, 2000, Clayoquot Sound was named and designated an official **United Nations Educational, Scientific and Cultural Organization Biosphere Reserve**. Clayoquot Sound is one of the 13 such designated areas in Canada; some 550 Biosphere Reserves exist around the world. To be named a UNESCO Biosphere Reserve, a region must show innovative approaches to conservation and sustainable development.

In order to be granted this status, residents of Clayoquot Sound submitted a comprehensive application to the UNESCO Man and Biosphere Program headquarters in Paris. This application needed to demonstrate a regional consensus by every community within the proposed boundary: a clear majority of individuals, special interest groups, local, provincial and federal governments -- even neighbouring communities outside the proposed Biosphere boundary. Achieving this consensus was an exhaustive process that took over seven years.

The Clayoquot Sound Biosphere Reserve consists of three zones: **The Core Zone** (110,281 hectares, 32%) is designated as an area where there is no general public use or activities other than the pursuit of further conservation objectives; **The Buffer Zone** (60,416 hectares, 17%) represents the area where research, monitoring and inventory initiatives are advanced and where limited commercial activity connected to eco-tourism may occur; and **The Transition Area** (179,250 hectares, 51%) where the main land use is related to tourism and tree harvesting and the main marine use is related to tourism and fisheries.

While the Biosphere Reserve designation has raised the profile of Clayoquot Sound in the international community, the designation does not offer any added protection from industrial logging of the ancient forests. Two different logging companies currently (late 2010) own Tree Farm Licences in Clayoquot Sound, carrying out industrial logging in some old growth forests.

For more information about industrial logging in Clayoquot Sound, contact the logging companies: **Iisaak Forestry**, 250-726-7037; **Coulson Forest Products**, 250-723-8118. For a different angle you can stop by the **Friends of Clayoquot Sound**'s office at 331 Neill Street or give them a call: 250-725-4218. For information about the Clayoquot Sound UNESCO Biosphere Reserve, contact the **Clayoquot Biosphere Trust**, 216 Main Street, 250-725-2219.

MEARES ISLAND

Stand anywhere on Main Street and look straight across the water to the green landmass ahead of you and most of what you see is Meares Island. The island is one of Tofino's dearest treasures, delivering its entire water supply, which is siphoned across Browning Passage through pipes laid along the sea bed.

Meares Island is known by three names. The name Meares comes from Captain John Meares, credited as the first European to discover the island. The island is located in Tla-o-qui-aht and Ahousaht First Nations Territory. The Tla-o-qui-aht call Meares Island *Wah-nah-juss* and the Ahousaht call it *Hilth-hoo-iss*.

In 1984, Meares Island was one of the early battlegrounds in the so-called War of the Woods. The Tla-o-qui-aht Tribal Council strategically declared most of the island a Tribal Park and gained an injunction against MacMillan Bloedel, the logging company preparing to log it. This injunction still stands and the island is jointly administered by the Tla-o-qui-aht and Ahousaht First Nations.

Meares Island's pristine beauty and its strategic, biological and cultural importance cannot be overstated. To fully experience all that Clayoquot Sound is, and all it has to offer, a visit to Meares is a must. We highly recommend you join a kayak eco-tour with an experienced and knowledgeable guide who can point out the many features of this island. At the very least, jump on a water taxi and hitch a ride over to the Big Tree Trail for an experience of a lifetime.

TOFINO GUIDE

For more information about getting to Meares Island, see **Meares Island Tours** (p. 96) and hiking the **Big Tree Trail** (p. 162). For more information about **Tla-o-qui-aht Tribal Parks**, see www.tribalparks.ca.

> "Meares Island is now known both nationally and internationally, largely due to a gallant fight, fought together in strong unity by two very different cultures--native and non-native--for a common cause. We believe in living in peace and harmony with nature and life itself. An immediate spinoff from Meares is unity, the ability of our two cultures to work together, which is a great start for future generations."
>
> Moses Martin, 1984
> Elected Chief, Tla-o-qui-aht First Nation

CULTURALLY MODIFIED TREES (CMT)

Foresters, archaeologists and Nuu-chah-nulth people refer to a tree or tree remnant with evidence of aboriginal use as a Culturally Modified Tree, or CMT. In our area, most CMTs are western red cedar. Many CMTs along our coast are large stumps. These stumps are evidence of trees felled many years ago with yew-wood axes and fire. The trees were then carved into canoes, or artfully hand split into cedar planks, called shakes.

Some CMTs in our area appear unscarred, but closer investigation reveals square holes chipped into them. These "test holes" are evidence that the Nuu-chah-nulth investigated that tree for use as a canoe, but for whatever reasons it failed the test and was left standing.

You may happen upon a younger western red cedar that has a long patch of bark missing up its trunk. This is recent evidence of a reclaimed Nuu-chah-nulth practice called bark stripping. A cut is made in the bark near the bottom of the tree and a long strip of bark is peeled up along the trunk. The bark is used to fabricate many different decorative and practical items like hats, mats and rope.

TOFINO GUIDE

NURSE LOGS

Clayoquot Sound is home to very large trees, and very stormy weather. This combination means that trees occasionally come crashing down, becoming an essential part of the forest's ecosystem as the logs gradually rot away.

A **nurse log** is created when seeds take root in the micro habitat of a fallen log; mosses and fungi and ferns appear first, then small shrubs and trees. As time passes all of this growth becomes increasingly dense and increasingly large. If you follow tree trunks in the forest to the ground, you will often find trees that are actually rooted to and growing around fallen logs that may have lain on the forest floor for centuries

The western red cedars make excellent candidates for long-lasting nurse logs because their wood is exceptionally rot resistant. Amazingly, the wood in these long-fallen logs can last through hundreds of years of rain, remaining solid enough to mill into saleable timber.

If you gaze long and hard into the forest, you may find an unusually straight line of closely-grouped thousand-year old trees. These giants likely got their start long ago on a straight nurse log, but have outlasted and overgrown their original host, as it finally succumbed to the rainforest's relentless, ever-creative process of decay.

TOP 10 MUST-SEE TREES OF CLAYOQUOT SOUND

1. **Eik Cedar Tree**
   - Western red cedar located across from Shelter Restaurant, near the highway as you enter Tofino. Believed to be 800-1000 years old, this tree was declared an insurance hazard in 2001 and ordered to be destroyed. The citizens mobilized, a media blitz raised awareness, two men made a home for 37 days in its canopy, and money was raised to fortify the tree with a kind of steel girdle, installed around the tree in 2002. For this and other actions Tofino was officially named Tree Hugging Capital of the World by friend and foe.

2. **Hanging Garden Tree**
   - Western red cedar on Meares Island's Big Tree Trail, about 600 metres into the trail, believed to be 1500-2000 years old

3. **Poster Tree**
   - Western red cedar on Meares Island's Big Tree Trail, about 500 metres into the trail, believed to be 1000-1500 years old.

4. **St. Columba Cedar**
   - Western red cedar on the grounds of St. Columba Church at Second Street and Main, believed to predate the church constructed next to it in 1913

TOP 10 MUST-SEE TREES OF CLAYOQUOT SOUND (cont.)

5. **Three Elders**
   - Western red cedars in a grouping near the tidal inlet's edge. Accessed through the Tofino Botanical Gardens (by admission, p. 207) down the boardwalk trail. The trees are believed to be between 500 and 800 years old.

6. **Florence Nightingale**
   - As it gradually decays, this remarkable nurse log is releasing rich nutrients to foster new growth. This tree has nursed so many new trees and plants that we have nicknamed her Florence Nightingale. If you hike the Spruce Fringe Trail (p. 132), you will walk directly under her. Her age is difficult to estimate in her current state, and the abundant life springing from her makes it hard to know if she is still living or if she is dead. Perhaps nurse logs never really die?

7. **The Silver Snag**
   - Just south of the southern sign welcoming you to the Pacific Rim National Park Reserve on the east side of the highway stands an 800-1000 year old silvered snag of what was once a mighty western red cedar. These grey dying tops of ancient living trees are known locally as **Grey Ghosts** (p. 137).

8. **Eagle Tree on Dead Man's Isle**
   - This aerie (nest site) located in a large Sitka spruce (*Picea sitchensis*) is a common stop on most whale watching expeditions. The resident eagles publicly nesting high on its branches don't seem to mind the attention as they raise their newborn eaglets each year.

9. **Ninth Hole Hemlock**
    - On the grounds of Long Beach Golf Course, 174 metres (192 yards, for golfers) from the white tee blocks at the ninth hole there is an often-cursed Western hemlock (*Tsuga heterophylla*). Save your best profanities for this resilient stalwart on the last hole.

10. **You Tell Us!**
    - If you see a remarkable tree that you think we should include in our Ten Must-See Trees of Clayoquot Sound, please contact us. If we agree, we'll print it in the *Tofino Guide* website (www.tofino-bc.com) and give you full credit, of course.

TOFINO'S TEMPERATE CLIMATE

We get a lot of drizzle here, but when it rains it pours

Tofino Climate Normals: 1971 - 2000

Coastal Temperate Rainforest

Storm Watching

20 Things to Do When it Rains

TOFINO GUIDE

WE GET A LOT OF DRIZZLE HERE, BUT WHEN IT RAINS IT POURS

Clayoquot Sound is one of the wettest places in North America.

How wet is wet? In 1995, Clayoquot Lake, 24 km from Tofino as the raven flies, received 6,460 millimetres (6.5 meters) of rainfall (for the Metrically Challenged, that's 7 yards, or 258 inches or 21.5 feet). This gives us the official designation of the soggiest location in North America where measurements are recorded.

Ironically, despite this wealth of fresh water, Tofino can experience water shortages during July and August at the height of our tourism season. Tofino's water source is the watershed of Mount Colnett, on Meares Island. Here, many streams contribute to various water lines that cross Browning Passage to the town of Tofino. Technically, there is never a water shortage in Tofino – but there can be a serious shortage of water storage facilities. This became nationally famous on the Labour Day Weekend of 2006, when media from all over Canada descended on Tofino to report that the town was officially closed due to a radically low municipal water supply. Thankfully, this has all been mitigated with a new water storage facility and an upgraded reservoir on Meares Island, near the source.

That being said, Tofino does ask that summer visitors never waste water. Most accommodation providers have water-saving measures in place, like low flush toilets and carefully scheduled garden irrigation.

The early pioneers believed that if there were clouds obscuring the summit of **Lone Cone on Meares Island** (p. 41), bad weather was approaching. If a ring of clouds surrounded the crown, then good weather was on its way. Today's residents have taken this legend one step further. A local saying goes something like this: **"Stand outside and face north to Lone Cone. If you cannot see Lone Cone, it is raining. If you can see Lone Cone it is about to rain."**

Residents may also tell you there's no such thing as bad weather, only bad clothing choices.

If you are confused by all of this, you can phone Tofino's weather station and speak to a real person, not just a recording, and you can learn the forecast – but only during regular business hours. The **Tofino Weather Station** is located at the **Tofino Airport** (250-725-3384), down Airport Road across from the Long Beach parking area (p. 130).

TOFINO GUIDE

Tofino Climate Normals: 1971 - 2000

		Jan	Feb	Mar	Apr	May	Jun	Jul	Aug	Sep	Oct	Nov	Dec	Year
Average high	°C	7.6	8.6	9.7	11.6	14.3	16.3	18.5	18.8	17.7	13.5	9.8	7.8	12.8
	°F	46	47	49	53	58	61	65	66	64	56	50	46	55
Record high	°C	20	19	18.3	22.8	27.6	32.2	32.8	32.8	29.4	23.9	21.1	15.6	32.8
	°F	68	66	64.9	73	82	90	91	91	85	75	70	60	91
Average low	°C	1.4	1.9	2.3	3.7	6.2	8.6	10.2	10.6	8.9	6	3.3	1.7	5.4
	°F	35	35	36	39	43	47	50	51	48	43	38	35	42
Record low	°C	-15	-9.2	-5.5	-1.7	-0.2	2.2	3.9	4.4	-0.6	-3.5	-12.7	-12.2	-15
	°F	5	15	22	29	32	36	39	40	31	26	9	10	5
Average Precipitation	mm	436	382	355	249	165	138	77	94	134	340	475	462	3,306
	in	17.1	15.0	14.0	9.8	6.5	5.4	3.0	3.7	5.3	13.4	18.7	18.2	130.2
Record Daily Precipitation	mm	174	184	170	126	96	83	98	131	106	154	155	166	
	in	6.9	7.3	6.7	5.0	3.8	3.3	3.9	5.2	4.2	6.1	6.1	6.6	

Source: Environment Canada: www.weatheroffice.gc.ca

COASTAL TEMPERATE RAINFOREST

Throughout this guide you will read the term **temperate rainforest**. Specific to our region, this type of forest is more accurately called a coastal temperate rainforest:

> Coastal temperate rain forests constitute a relatively rare forest type, originally covering less than 1/5 of 1% of the earth's land surface. Three features are common to all coastal temperate rain forests: proximity to oceans, the presence of mountains, and as a result of the two, high rainfall. Therefore they are restricted to the coastal margins of western North America, New Zealand, Tasmania, Chile and Argentina, as well as portions of Japan, northwest Europe and the Black Sea coast of Turkey and Georgia. Over half of these coastal temperate rain forests worldwide have been extirpated due to logging and conversion to other non-forest uses. Of those that remain, the largest undeveloped tracts are found in South America and North America. In North America, no intact, unlogged watersheds of any size remain in the continental United States. **The largest areas of undeveloped coastal temperate rain forests** in the more productive zone of this biome **exist in British Columbia**.

(excerpted from: *Coastal Temperate Rain Forests: Ecological Characteristics, Status and Distribution Worldwide*, Ecotrust and Conservation International, 1992)

A simple definition of coastal temperate rainforest might read: **Not too hot, not too cold. Lots of rain. Between the mountains and the ocean. Big trees and lots of green squishy stuff.**

TOFINO GUIDE

The major tree species in our area of coastal temperate rainforest are western hemlock, western red cedar, Sitka spruce, and Douglas fir. The high forest canopy is thickly matted with mosses, lichens and epiphytes (plants that are rooted on and derive their nutrients from other plants). Look up, way up, when you are hiking through the forest and you will see these mats, hovering like mini-ecosystems in the trees.

STORM WATCHING

Imagine: You are walking on the beach, into a wind so powerful it is pushing you backwards. The sound of the crashing surf, even at low tide, has become so deafening that you have to shout just to be heard. You can taste the salt whipping off the top of rooster-tailed waves. The rain is intense, but you are warm and dry in your rubber rain gear that the resort has provided. The wind is blowing you back so hard now that you decide to lean forward on your toes, arms outstretched, and dip your entire body 45 degrees to the ground. You feel like are flying. You scream and holler, but the howling wind is so loud, your partner can barely hear you.

Alternatively: You are inside by the glowing fire, in the comfort of your hotel. With your drink in hand you marvel at the power of the rain pelting your window. You mark the fluctuating speed of the wind as its pitch rises and falls like a child blowing a whistle. You take a sip of your drink, watching crazed people clad in yellow rubber from head-to-toe, leaning forward into the storm.

This is storm watching, a pastime that has become so popular that people monitor the weather in order to try to catch a last minute storm. The trend officially started in 1996, when the Wickaninnish Inn (p. 223) began marketing a Storm Watchers' package. Thus began an audacious form of West Coast promotion: embracing the worst of the winter's weather as a means to bring people -- and tourism revenue -- to Tofino in the slow winter season. Have a look at every resort's winter marketing strategy now and you will see that the technique has caught on. Laugh if you will, but when you get out in a storm and feel the raw power of the Pacific, it is easy to understand the fascination.

TOFINO GUIDE

20 THINGS TO DO WHEN IT RAINS

First, stop complaining! Remember, you came to a rainforest and those trees would not exist without lots and lots of water. If you did not bring rain gear, visit the Co-op Grocery, Stormlight Marine Outfitters, Tofino Sea Kayaking, Method Marine, or Tofino Fishing and Trading, where you can pick up waterproof provisions. If you are lucky, you may find used waterproof gear at Castaways Secondhand Scores.

Second, measure it! No scientific gauge necessary, any old pot will do. Afterwards you can brag about how much rain you collected. Can you beat the single day record downfall of 184 mm (7.2 inches) that came pelting down on February 24, 1982?

1. Wait out the rainstorm inside one of the covered slide tunnels in the playground at the Village Green (Warning: tunnels can become quite crowded).

2. If you're going to be wet anyway, rent a wetsuit and go surfing or snorkelling.

3. Get a tarp from the Co-op Hardware store, go to Comber's Beach and make an ocean and rain observation tent.

4. Go out for a walk! There are two fairly sheltered trails in the National Park that are mostly boardwalk (read: no mud) and they go deep into the forest where the canopy will act much like an umbrella. Try the Rain Forest Trail (A or B) or the Spruce Fringe Trail for the best cover.

5. Imitate a duck. This is fun for the whole family!

6. Visit the Wickaninnish Interpretive Centre.

7. Pick a street and do the Gene Kelly Thing, "Singing in the Rain."

8. Have a latte at one of the many coffee shops and cafés.

9. Go on a whale watching tour in a covered aluminum boat or zodiac (for the latter you will want to be well rain-geared).

10. Go swimming in one of the indoor pools at Ocean Village Resort or MacKenzie Beach Resort.

11. Check out the displays at the Raincoast Interpretive Centre in the Tofino Botanical Gardens.

12. Rent a video at Groovy Movie or the LA Grocery.

13. Visit the volunteer-run Maritime Museum.

14. Go for a pint of beer at one of Tofino's pubs and watch the clouds dance over or envelop Meares Island.

15. Do local research and surf the Web at the public library to plan your next activities.

16. Catch a lecture or film at the Green Point Campground's Theatre.

17. Grab an umbrella and hike down to Tonquin Beach to watch ill-prepared youthful squatters raising tarps as they curse the weather in different languages.

18. Visit the Tofino art galleries.

19. Email your friends and family to tell them just how sunny and dry Tofino is.

20. Go post card shopping which is sure to brighten your day since every post card only shows Tofino and Long Beach baking in the sunshine.

TOFINO'S BEACHES

Beachcombing

Can we build a campfire on the beach?

Tonquin Beach

MacKenzie Beach

Chesterman Beach and Frank Island

Cox Bay

Top 10 Beaches of Clayoquot Sound

BEACHCOMBING

For the best treasures, you have to get up early before everything is picked over by birds and your fellow tourists. Sand dollars, sea urchin shells, and beach shells can be fairly easy to find but make sure the living creatures inside have already vacated before you move them.

If you are turning over rocks to admire the small creatures underneath, please gently replace the rocks you have removed, in the same position and the same way up. This protects eggs and other small organisms on the underside of the rock.

After hours of beachcombing, look at your treasures and ask yourself if you really should take these things home. We strongly advise you to leave them on the beach.

Watch for posted signs about beachcombing within the Pacific Rim National Park Reserve (all beaches south of Cox Bay, including Long Beach). **The removal of driftwood and shells is prohibited in the park, and in any location it is illegal to remove living creatures without a proper license** (p. 185 for information on shellfish licenses).

The most sought-after beach items are the elusive **Japanese Glass Balls**. These are old fish net floats, and they have been floating on the Pacific Ocean for decades. Finding them is a rare excitement. Glass ball beachcombing becomes easier the further from civilization you travel. Your best bet is after a winter storm on any remote stretch of sand between here and Cape Scott on the farthest northern point of Vancouver Island – best of luck getting there.

CAN WE BUILD A CAMPFIRE ON THE BEACH?

Before you build a campfire on a beach, check for restrictions on British Columbia's **Wildfire Management Branch** website (www.bcwildfire.ca) or call their automated information service and follow the prompts: 888-336-7378.

Campfires on beaches are permitted on all beaches in Tofino and the Pacific Rim National Park Reserve with the following exceptions:

- No fires are permitted on Cox Bay

- No fires are permitted between Green Point and Esowista village on Long Beach

The following restrictions are usually in place for campfires in Tofino and the Pacific Rim National Park Reserve:

- The campfire must be under 0.6 metres (2 feet) wide and under 0.6 metres high

- Campfires should be under the obvious high tide line and at least 3 metres from vegetation or driftwood

- Campfires must be completely extinguished after their use

- No campfires are permitted between 11 pm and 6 am

It is illegal to burn driftwood or any other beach material. You can **purchase firewood** and kindling at all of the campground offices (p. 237) and the two gas stations (p. 248) in town.

TOFINO GUIDE

The following beaches are located in the District of Tofino and do not require a Park Pass for use or parking. We start at Tonquin Beach at northern tip of the peninsula and move south to Cox Bay, near the southern boundary between the District of Tofino and the beginning of Pacific Rim National Park Reserve.

TONQUIN BEACH

Tonquin Beach is the first of four accessible hiking beaches located within the District of Tofino, outside of the national park. The parking lot at the trailhead is less than 1 km from the Post Office, an easy and pleasant walk. To get there, head for the end of Tonquin Park Road, and from there follow a winding boardwalk through the forest for about 7 minutes. You'll be walking through a nature preserve set aside by the District of Tofino. After descending about 75 steps, you will be at the beach. Although it is not very large, this beach feels secluded and has the advantage of getting full sun.

When the boardwalk on the Tonquin Trail is wet – and this is true of all boardwalks – the planks can become very slippery, especially in the early morning or during and after rain showers. So watch your step carefully.

After arriving on the beach, look out to Wickaninnish Island (straight out and a bit to your left) and Felice Island (off to your right, also called Round Island). If your timing is right, you will experience the region's best view of the summer sunset.

Tonquin Beach is named after the 19th century American trading vessel *Tonquin*. In 1811 the vessel sank near here in appalling circumstances. Following a trading altercation, a number of First Nations people boarded the vessel and killed most of the 35 member crew. The following day they returned to the vessel and a surviving crew member ignited the powder kegs on board, killing himself and all the local people who had come aboard. The ship sank without a trace and the wreck has not yet been discovered. It is one of the most mysterious and sought-after wrecks on the West Coast, still attracting keen divers and treasure seekers.

In September 2003 *The New York Times* detailed the discovery of an early 19th century anchor snagged by a local crab fisherman and raised by a team of local divers. This anchor may belong to the *Tonquin* but shifting sands have yet to reveal the wreck itself.

For more information about the wreck of the *Tonquin*, purchase a copy of *Tonquin: The Ghostship of Clayoquot Sound*, a booklet written by David W. Griffiths, a local marine archaeologist. The booklet is available at Tofino Sea Kayaking, 320 Main Street.

Hiking Time
About 7 minutes (one way) from the parking lot

Length
A few hundred metres, then return

Location
From Post Office, travel south on First Street, past the hospital and a small park. Turn right on Arnet Street, then left up Tonquin Park Road to a small parking lot on the left at the end of the road.

Difficulty
Very easy, short steep ascent on concrete path, then all boardwalk. One descent of about 75 stairs

MACKENZIE BEACH

MacKenzie Beach is definitely worth a visit, particularly if you are with small children. Longer and more spectacular beaches exist, but here the beach is generally less windy, the waves are gentler and calmer, and it is family friendly. There are four resorts and two campgrounds adjacent to this beach, but none of this detracts from its calm beauty.

A fun low tide adventure will have you exploring the rocky intertidal zone at the far left (south) end of the beach. At a very low tide you'll find multicoloured ochre sea stars (*Pisaster ochraceus* or, to the kids, purple and orange starfish), many different species of limpets (small, pointy capped shells, in kid talk), aggregating anemones (*Anthopleura elegantissima* or, to the kids, greenish jelly blobs with alien-like tentacles) and lots more squishy slimy sea stuff. Kids love this beach for its relatively warm water, easy access, friendly waves and the many exploration opportunities in the southern rocky section. Adults with small kids love it because here they can be a bit easier about their children's safety than at the bigger beaches in the area – although please always be cautious and keep a very close watch on your small beach explorers, no matter which beach you choose.

Location
Head south out of town, watch for the **Tin Wis Resort Best Western** sign at a sharp corner. Just after the Tin Wis sign you'll see Hellesen Drive (3.7 km from the Post Office). Turn right on Hellesen and go to the end of the road.

What to do if you see a…

BALD EAGLE

Get used to it -- bald eagles (*Haliaeetus leucocephalus*) are common in Tofino and the surrounding areas. If you are out on the water with a whale watching charter, you will likely make a brief stop adjacent to a local bald eagle aerie (nest site). This aerie has been occupied for about 20 years, reportedly by the same couple. Two or three chicks are born yearly, and if you are lucky enough to be witnessing this in the spring you may catch sight of the young eaglets poking their heads above the 2-metre wide nest.

If you are really interested in seeing a lot of eagles, head out to the regional landfill where there are regularly up to 50 bald eagles searching for easy food. This is also a great spot to find eagle feathers, but **do not try to bring an eagle feather over the USA border**: an eagle feather law in the USA prohibits their possession unless you are a Native American. The consequence for bringing home your treasure could be as much as a $25,000 fine.

TOFINO GUIDE

CHESTERMAN BEACH AND FRANK ISLAND

When asked, "What's a good beach to go for a walk on?" most locals immediately say "Chesterman.". Frank Island splits this long and lovely beach into two sections: North and South Chesterman. We will start you walking at the North Chesterman parking lot.

After taking a very short trail from the parking lot (see Location, below) through massive Sitka spruce trees, you'll arrive at **North Chesterman Beach**. Look to your right (north) and you'll see two buildings belonging to the Wickaninnish Inn. Here you'll find a relatively unknown and welcome treat: **Driftwood Café**, a small coffee and sandwich outlet located in the bottom level of the **Wickaninnish Inn**. The public is welcome to walk right in off the beach for an exceptional coffee, lunch or snack. This is a great opportunity to enter one of British Columbia's most prestigious hotels without going through the front door as a guest or going to its upscale restaurant.

Standing at the north end of the beach, look straight out to sea at a low or medium tide and you will see a group of large rocks on the beach. Head down to scramble around them if you want some fun, rocky exploration before beginning your trek along the beach. Now start walking to the left (south) and you will be gazing at **Frank Island**. The route to Frank Island takes you along a **tombolo**, a narrow sandspit connected to an island. Tide permitting, you should take the time to explore the tide pools and rock crevices around its outer edges. Above the high tide line is private land with occupied cabins. Please respect the private property boundary rope and signs. Be very careful not to find yourself cut off on any of these beach rocks or islands by an incoming tide.

From Frank Island continue south along **South Chesterman Beach**. The beach ends at a rocky outcrop separating Chesterman Beach from **Rosie Bay**. At an extremely low tide you can access Rosie Bay and some really fun tidal caves, but a tide this low is rare. Check your tide chart to see if you can time the trip appropriately. Please be aware that all of the land above the high tide line at Rosie Bay is private. Only hike over to Rosie Bay when it is accessible via the low tide route. Now retrace your steps along the beach to the parking lot at North Chesterman.

Location

Head south out of town, watch for the **Beaches Grocery** shopping complex on the left (east) side of the road. Just after Beaches Grocery you will see Lynn Road on your right (4.3 km from the Post Office). Turn right on Lynn Road. After 300 metres you will come to a T-intersection, with a parking lot straight ahead. Park here.

TOFINO GUIDE

COX BAY

Cox Bay straddles the boundary of the Pacific Rim National Park Reserve and the District of Tofino. It is the final beach as you head out of town before you reach the national park. There are three resorts located at the north end of the beach: Pacific Sands Resort, Cox Bay Beach Resort and Long Beach Lodge.

There are two public access trails to Cox Bay described on page 104. For hiking purposes, your best bet is to use the public access at the Cox Bay Beach Resort across the road from the **Cox Bay Visitor Centre**. Park in the free public parking area and walk the short boardwalk trail to the beach. There are bathroom and shower facilities at the parking lot. If this parking lot is full, go across the highway to the Visitor Centre where parking is also free.

Standing at the edge of the trail, take notice of the activity surrounding you. Surfers, sandcastle architects, dog walkers and Frisbee throwers will fill the scene with action. Remember this scene so you can contrast it to the calmer, southern end of the beach.

If the tide is low, head north (right) from the boardwalk to the rocky headland at the water's edge. If the tide is low enough you will be able to explore the shallow caves in the rocks facing the ocean. Children will have fun plunging into the craggy forest and underbrush above these rocks. Find one of the many criss-crossed trails and wander around with your children. Be warned that there are steep drops and the potential for ocean surges near the edges of these rocks (see *Rogue Waves*, p. 11). **Do not leave kids unattended**.

Now walk south along the beach towards Cox Point, the long forested finger of land pointing west. If you are walking close to the forest you will see the other public access trail to Cox Bay about half way down the beach. There is a composting toilet facility beside this trail, about 20 metres from the beach. Soon after you pass this trail, notice the sign that marks the boundary of the Pacific Rim National Park Reserve.

Approaching the rocks at the south end of the beach you will notice a distinct change in your surroundings. No groups of people gather here, like at the north end; the feeling is much calmer here. Enjoy this relative solitude while you examine the many pockets of small, smooth oval-shaped rocks, looking for sea glass that has been polished by the Pacific.

As you return to the north end of the beach, do not be tempted to take the middle trail to create a loop back to the Cox Bay Beach Resort Parking lot. There is no trail along the highway back to your car, and the sharp curves in the highway create dangerous walking conditions. It is much more pleasant to continue down the beach to the same public access trail you arrived on.

Length
Cox Bay is about 1.5 km long, so the entire hike, including the boardwalk, is about 3 km.

Location
From the Post Office, travel south 6.9 km, just past the Cox Bay Visitor Centre. Turn right into Cox Bay Beach Resort, which is a shared access with Long Beach Lodge. Immediately veer right towards Cox Bay Beach Resort. There is no public beach access to Cox Bay through Long Beach Lodge or through Pacific Sands Resort.

Difficulty
Very easy. There are no steps on the boardwalk trail, although there is a steep ramp made out of soft sand at the beach-end of the trial, making unassisted wheelchair access difficult.

TOFINO GUIDE

TOP 10 BEACHES OF CLAYOQUOT SOUND

All times and distances are one-way from Tofino

1. **Long Beach** (of course), Pacific Rim National Park Reserve
   - 16 km in length
   - White sand, adjacent old growth forests, notable length
   - Accessible by parking lots and trails

2. **Florencia Bay**, Pacific Rim National Park Reserve (Wreck Bay)
   - 3.5 km in length
   - White sand, cliffs of clay, crescent shape
   - Accessible by nearby parking area and trails

3. **Ahous Bay**, Vargas Island
   - 2.5 km in length
   - White sand, grey whale feeding site, remarkable hidden estuary
   - Accessible by boat, (about 30 minutes) kayak (at least four hours) or over-flown by seaplane (less than 10 minutes)

4. **Cow Bay**, Flores Island
   - 2 km in length
   - White sand, grey whale feeding site, almost tropically colourful waters
   - Accessible by boat (about 1 hour), kayak (a long day trip) or over-flown by seaplane (12 minutes)

5. **Radar Beach**, Pacific Rim National Park Reserve
   - 1.75 km in length
   - White sand, impressive headlands, crescent shape, challenging hike
   - Accessible by trail

6. **Whaler Island Beach**, Between Vargas and Flores Islands
   - 0.5 km in length
   - A small island almost entirely covered with white sand, historical significance to First Nations whaling tradition, relatively difficult access
   - Accessible by boat (about 25 minutes), kayak (about a four hour paddle) or over-flown by seaplane (about 10 minutes): See Canadian Hydrographic Service Nautical Chart #3673 for location

7. **Cox Bay**, 7 km south of Tofino
   - 1.5 km in length
   - White sand, large surf, caves at low tide.
   - Pacific Sands Resort, Long Beach Lodge and Cox Bay Beach Resort are located here
   - Accessible by car and trail

8. **Chesterman Beach**, both south and north sections, 4.5 km south of Tofino
   - 2.5 km in length, if you include a walk out to Frank Island at a low tide
   - White sand. Numerous residents and their dogs cruising around.
   - Residential and vacation homes are located here.
   - accessible by car and bike path

Tofino's Beaches

TOFINO GUIDE

TOP 10 BEACHES OF CLAYOQUOT SOUND (cont.)

9. **South Beach**, Pacific Rim National Park Reserve
   - 0.2 km in length
   - Small pebbles make a jingly whooshing noise as the waves roll in and out
   - A narrow channel helps create the largest waves of all
   - Accessible by trail from Wickaninnish Interpretive Centre

10. **Combers Beach**, Pacific Rim National Park Reserve
    - 3 km in length
    - White sand with a river crossing, tidal erosion and driftwood galore
    - Accessible by parking lot

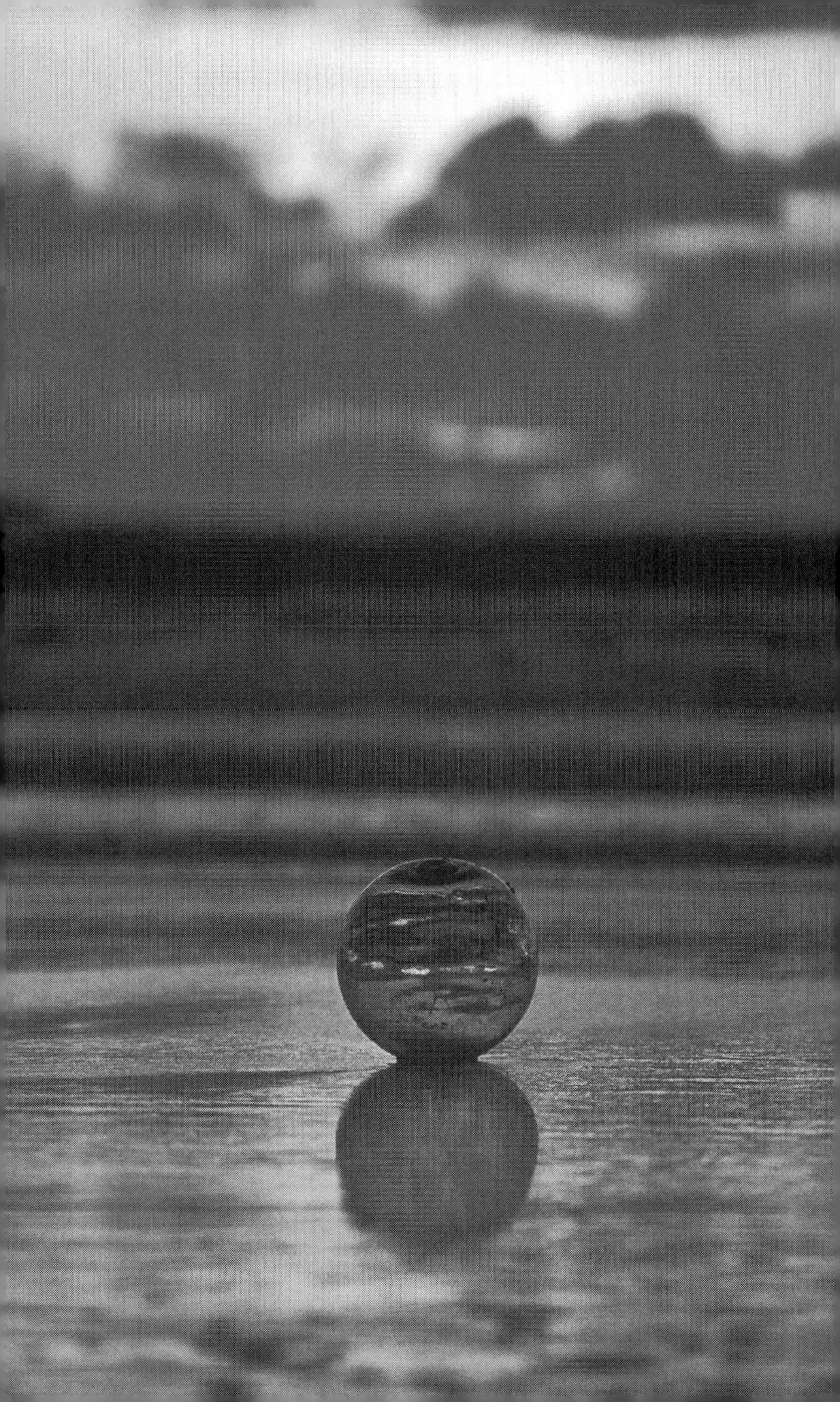

PACIFIC RIM NATIONAL PARK RESERVE

About Pacific Rim National Park Reserve

Fees at Pacific Rim National Park Reserve

Wickaninnish Interpretive Centre

Green Point Theatre

Wheelchair Accessibility in Pacific Rim National Park Reserve

Top 10 Activities in the Pacific Rim National Park Reserve

ABOUT PACIFIC RIM NATIONAL PARK RESERVE

Located on the west coast of Vancouver Island, Pacific Rim National Park Reserve consists of three units: Long Beach, Broken Group Islands, and the West Coast Trail. The Long Beach Unit is the best known and most accessible of the three park units. The most famous feature of the Long Beach Park Unit is of course Long Beach, which stretches for 16 kilometres (10 miles) between Florencia Bay and Schooner Cove. **For more on Long Beach, see page 130**.

The Long Beach Unit comprises 13,715 hectares (137 square kilometres). Of this area, 7,690 hectares is terrestrial, covering a variety of ecosystems: rainforest, bogs, beaches and small lakes. A marine component of the Long Beach Unit comprises 6,025 hectares, reaching out almost 3 kilometres offshore in places. This protects the coast's rocky islets, which are vital sea lion haul-outs and bird nesting sites.

In the late 1960s, Howard McDiarmid, the local doctor and MLA (Member of the Legislature) who later founded the Wickaninnish Inn (p. 223), lobbied energetically for the creation of the national park. On the recommendation of Jean Chretien, then Minister of Indian Affairs and Northern Development, the Pacific Rim National Park was created in 1970. The park is the core protected area within the Clayoquot Sound UNESCO Biosphere Reserve.

FEES AT PACIFIC RIM NATIONAL PARK RESERVE

To enjoy the Pacific Rim National Park Reserve and its facilities, you will need to pay an entry and service fee. This is a year-round policy. According to Parks Canada, revenues from entry and service fees "support visitor services and facilities. This means that every time you visit a park or site you are investing in its future — and in a legacy for future generations." This fee is generally referred to as a Park Pass.

You can purchase a Park Pass the following locations:

- Payment machines located at almost every parking lot within the Park (**credit card only, some machines may not be in service through the winter**)
- Any of the three Visitor Centres (p. 25)
- The entrance to Green Point Campground (p. 237)
- The Wickaninnish Interpretive Centre (p. 79)

The receipt you receive doubles as your Park Pass, and should be placed in a visible location in your vehicle. If you are not travelling by car it is difficult to know where or how to display your Pass, but technically you are still obliged to purchase one if you are not travelling with a vehicle. The Park Pass entitles you to park in any designated parking area within the Park and to use all of the Park's trails and facilities, including the Wickaninnish Interpretive Centre (p. 79). The parking areas are patrolled by officials checking for valid Park Passes on the dashboards of vehicles within the Park.

Beach Walk Pass

This entitles the purchaser to vehicle parking at any of the two Long Beach parking areas (p. 130), use of the picnic facilities and **access to Long Beach for up to four hours**. This pass does not include any facilities or areas outside of Long Beach, so purchase a Park Pass if you are planning on visiting the Wickaninnish Interpretive Centre or any other areas in the Park.

Fee Schedule for Park Passes at the Pacific Rim National Park Reserve

	Day Pass	Beach Walk	Annual Pass
Adult	$ 7.80	$ 4.90	$ 39.20
Senior	$ 6.80	$ 4.30	$ 34.30
Youth	$ 3.90	$ 2.50	$ 19.60
Family/Group	$ 19.60	$ 12.25	$ 98.10
Commercial Group, per person	$ 6.80		
School Groups, per student	$ 2.90		

Park Pass Structure

Adult: Person 17 to 64 years of age

Senior: Person 65 years of age or over

Youth: Person 6 to 16 years of age

Family/Group: Up to seven people with a maximum of two adults arriving in a single vehicle.

School Groups: Students of elementary and secondary schools.

WICKANINNISH INTERPRETIVE CENTRE

Originally the site of a hotel that accommodated guests for several decades before the advent of Pacific Rim National Park Reserve, the centre is now home to a museum, restaurant, and theatre. This attractive building is most certainly worth a few hours of exploring, especially if exciting weather drives you indoors.

It's best to visit the centre early in your trip, for everything you see there will help you to appreciate more fully the natural and cultural intricacies of this area. There are several displays on aboriginal life including a large traditional native canoe carved by a 90 year old elder. The life-size whale display is impressive, especially for children who will appreciate the sense of scale that is conveyed when they stand near it.

Every 60 minutes or so, you can view an educational movie inside a small theatre near the Centre's entrance.

Don't miss the upstairs where there are more displays on wildlife, ongoing park studies in progress as well as a lookout nook where you can idly watch for passing whales (this is best with binoculars). If you're with toddlers, don't miss the upstairs play area.

The family friendly, full service **Wickaninnish Restaurant** is open for lunch and dinner. Perched over the Pacific Ocean, the restaurant has one of the best views of any restaurant in the area (p. 82 for a full description of the restaurant). The Centre is also at the head of the trail leading to **South Beach** (p. 142) and **Wickaninnish Trail** (p. 144).

Admission to the Wickaninnish Interpretive Centre is included with your Pacific Rim National Park Reserve Park Pass.

Location

27.9 km from the Post Office to the Wick Road, watching for the Wickaninnish Interpretive Centre sign. Turn right (west) down

Wick Road, then drive 2.7 km to the parking lot at the end of the road. Stay left along the way and watch for the large Wickaninnish Interpretive Centre signs.

Operating Hours

10.30 am to 6 pm, seven days a week

GREEN POINT THEATRE

Beginning late June and continuing most nights until September, this theatre hosts speakers, lectures, and films. This highly recommended after-dinner activity takes place in a building designed to look like a traditional Nuu-chah-nulth Bighouse.

The events are arranged by the Pacific Rim National Park Reserve. Watch the schedule posted around town and in the current issue of *Tofino Time* for upcoming events. Some of the best presentations have focused on the migrating grey whales, the black bear, erosion in the park and shipwrecks. Admission and parking is included with your Park Pass. Washrooms are available on-site.

Location
20.4 km from the Post Office at the Green Point Campground turnoff. Turn right off the Pacific Rim Highway. Advance tickets are available at the camp kiosk.

Doors open at 7.30 pm nightly and shows start promptly at 8:00 pm

WHEELCHAIR ACCESSIBILITY IN PACIFIC RIM NATIONAL PARK RESERVE

Wickaninnish Interpretive Centre
- Theatre and exhibits
- All-terrain wheelchairs (manually operated by a companion or user operated) are available on loan.
- Accessible washrooms

Wickaninnish Area
- Shorepine Bog Trail (1 km, boardwalk) - Picnic area
- First 300 m of the Nuu-chah-nulth Trail

Bog Trail Boardwalk
- Accessible washrooms
- Trail and Picnic area

Green Point Campground
- Theatre
- Viewpoint
- Green Point Drive-In Campground (accessible washroom)

Long Beach
- Day Use Areas
- Accessible washrooms
- Picnic area
- Beach accesses (dependent on tides and beach log distribution)

Radar Hill Viewpoint
- Viewing platform
- Accessible toilet

TOFINO GUIDE

TOP 10 ACTIVITIES IN THE PACIFIC RIM NATIONAL PARK RESERVE

1. **Visit Long Beach**
   - Go surfing, boogie boarding or take a really long hike.

2. **Hike to Schooner Cove**
   - Be sure you make it to the beach

3. **Go to the Wickaninnish Interpretive Centre**
   - Entrance to the centre is included with your Park Pass. If you have kids, go upstairs to the play area

4. **Eat on the patio at the Wickaninnish Restaurant**
   - We dare you to try to find a better view that is open to the public, provides seating, has a liquor license and where you can watch surfers entertaining you out front.

5. **Hike the Bog Trail**
   - Find the carnivorous sundew plant (*Drosera rotundifolia*) after you read about it in the excellent interpretive booklet that you remembered to pick up at the beginning of the trail. You read that right – it's a plant that eats animals! (Well, little ones...)

6. **Hike the Rain Forest Trail**
   - Walk across a stream on a 15 metre-long bridge crafted out of one cedar tree (that is on Loop B – Loop A is equally beautiful but without the log bridge).

7. **View a Presentation at the Green Point Theatre**
    - Find a schedule in the current *Tofino Time* magazine and head out to Green Point Campground to enjoy a presentation in the theatre by Parks Canada staff or a local researcher. The presentation will be about any number of local natural history phenomena.

8. **Visit Florencia (Wreck) Bay**
    - Craft a clay bowl out of the grey clay in the cliffs that frame the beach. Imagine the history here: over 100 years ago gold-seekers flocked here to sluice the sands for gold. Sadly, no one got rich.

9. **Go Golfing**
    - Long Beach Golf Course is located within the Pacific Rim National Park Reserve. It is a well-kept little course with challenging fairways and friendly staff.

10. **Salute the Sunset on a Radar Hill Platform**
    - Take in the stunning 180 degree views of the Pacific Ocean, beach and rainforest.

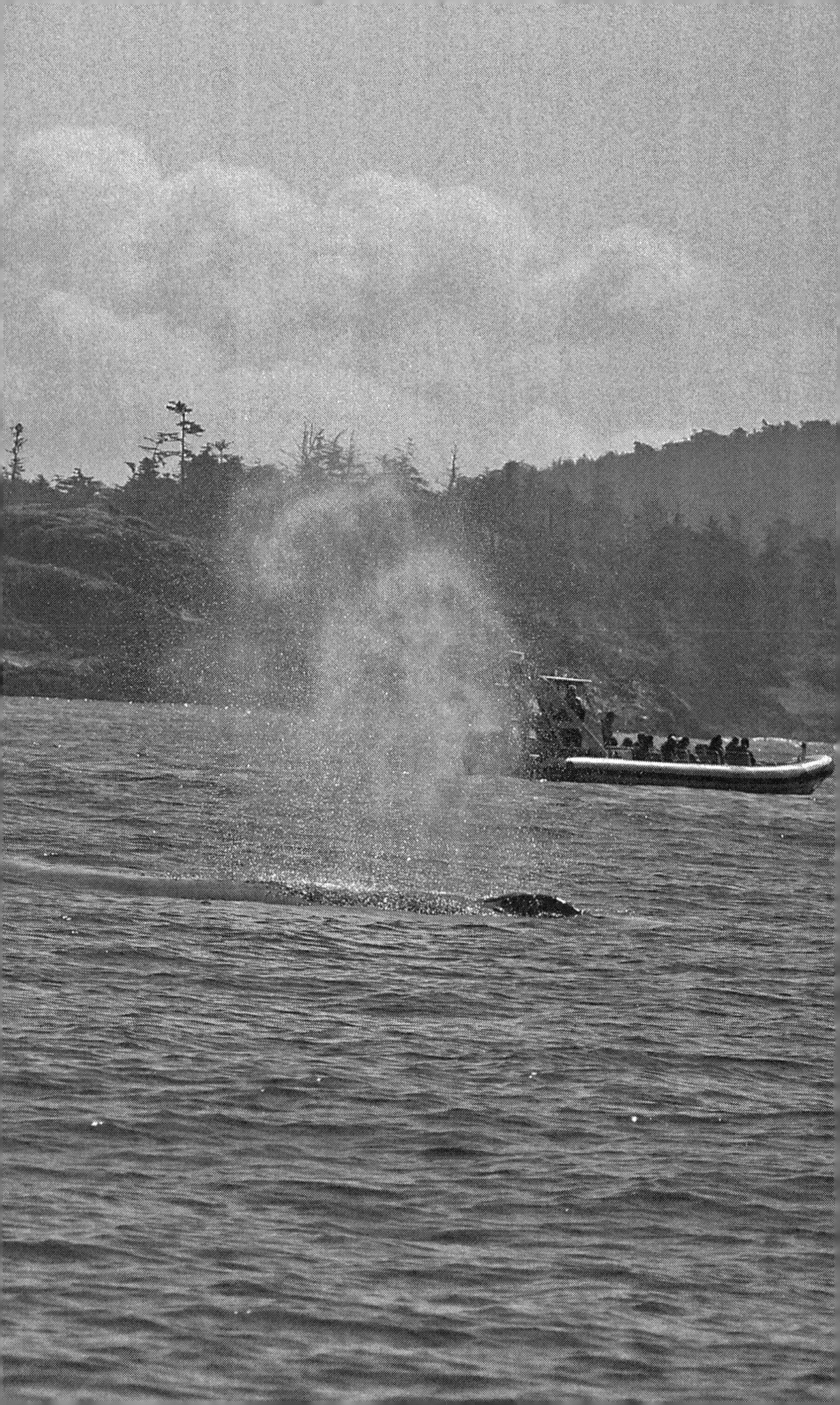

CHARTERS & TOURS

Whale Watching

Bear Watching

Hot Springs Tours

Birdwatching

Cultural Tours

Scenic Boat Charters

Scenic Flights

Sea Kayaking

Sport Fishing

SCUBA Diving

TOFINO GUIDE

WHALE WATCHING

Whale watching in Tofino is a year round activity, but the season officially begins in March with the Pacific Rim Whale Festival. Whale watching from shore is not a viable option, unless you have very good binoculars and tremendous patience and/or a hefty dose of good fortune. Fortunately for whale lovers, a number of different companies will take you out whale watching. Most companies offer the option of going out in an open Zodiac-type of boat or in a covered aluminum craft. **Ask the tour company about which type of vessel is best suited to your party**.

Most whale watching trips last between 2-3 hours. You can expect to see grey whales during your trip and possibly humpback whales. You will likely encounter bald eagles, harbour seals, Steller sea lions, possibly sea otters and, if you are very lucky, orca whales. The price and policies for adults and children wishing to go whale watching in Tofino vary according to vessel type, trip length and services offered. You can find departure times throughout the day including sunset whale cruises.

Folks with bad backs or small bladders should definitely avoid the Zodiac tours, which can be very bumpy. If you are prone to sea sickness you can purchase anti-nausea pills at the **Tofino Pharmacy** (360 Campbell Street, 250-725-3101). Ask the whale watching charter company about different methods to avoid sea sickness.

Adventure Tofino
615 Pfeiffer Cr, 250-725-2895, www.adventuretofino.com

Clayoquot Eco-Tours at the Whale Centre
411 Campbell Street, 888-474-2288 or 250-725-2132,
www.tofinowhalecentre.com

Jamie's Whaling Station
606 Campbell Street, 800-667-9913 or 250-725-3919,
www.jamies.com

Ocean Outfitters
368 Main Street, 877-906-2326 or 250-725-2866,
www.oceanoutfitters.bc.ca

Remote Passages Marine Excursions
51 Wharf Street, 800-666-9833 or 250-725-3330,
www.remotepassages.com

Weigh West Marine Resort
634 Campbell Street, 800-665-8922 or 250-725-3277,
www.weighwest.com

West Coast Aquatic Safaris
101-A Fourth Street, 877-594-2537 or 250-725-9227,
www.whalesafaris.com

TOFINO GUIDE

What to do if you see a...

SEA OTTER

Count yourself lucky and prepare to be charmed as you watch them swim on their backs snacking on sea urchins or crab or shellfish. Sea otters (*Enhydra lutris*) nearly became extinct due to rampant overhunting in the 19th century, when tens of thousands of animals were slaughtered for their valuable pelts. Between 1969 and 1972 about one hundred sea otters were captured in Alaska and reintroduced in Kyuquot Sound, on the north-western coast of Vancouver Island. The population grew quickly, and today they are often seen as far south as Tofino. Interestingly, their numbers have increased to the point that on some areas of the West Coast they are now considered a menace. Their large appetite for crabs, clams and other commercially harvested shellfish have decimated local populations of certain species along the coast. The northern abalone is one of the sea otter's favourite meals. This creates a fascinating conundrum for conservationists, where both predator and prey are recovering from near extinction and both are protected under Canada's Species at Risk Act.

BEAR WATCHING

Clayoquot Sound is home to a large number of resident black bears. Most whale watching outfitters have ocean-going tours that specialise in seeing bears in their own environment. On these bear watching expeditions, you will see them ambling along the beaches as they forage for food, while you remain at a safe distance in the boat. One of the advantages of black bear tours is that the boats generally travel in protected water around Meares Island where the ocean swell is minimal. On a calm day, the ocean can be as smooth as glass, providing exceptional opportunities for nature photography as well as close encounters with bears.

Also expect to see eagles, seals, sea lions and other wildlife as you cruise along the shoreline. This trip is different from whale watching, as the emphasis is directed to land mammals and the boat remains close to shore. Bear watching tours are around 2-3 hours with rates similar to whale watching. Expect wonderful photographic opportunities, especially rewarding if you have a large lens.

Recommended time of the year for bear watching is late spring through early October. It is possible to see bears at other times of the year on a charter, but always ask the tour operator ahead of time about the likelihood of glimpsing bears, to avoid disappointment.

The whale watching companies listed above all offer bear watching tours.

Browning Pass Charters specializes in bear watching tours: 250-725-2618, www.browningpass.com

HOT SPRINGS TOURS

This is a year-round adventure with most charter outfits leaving in the morning and picking up in the late afternoon. The best part about this trip is that, weather permitting, the tour can often take on elements of a whale watching trip, with the destination of hot springs at the end.

Hot Springs Cove is about **30 km north of Tofino**. The trailhead to the hot springs is about a one hour and 20 minute boat ride from Tofino. Passengers are dropped off here, and to reach the hot springs you follow a long boardwalk that meanders through an old growth cedar forest for about 25-30 minutes. You may see the steam before you glimpse the geothermal springs coming out of the ground at about 50 degrees Celsius. A small, steaming stream cascades down a waterfall into a series of soaking pools naturally cut out of the rocks. The pools of the hot springs are large enough to hold three or four people at once, and they step down a natural course, right to the edge of the cool Pacific Ocean. This combination creates one of the most treasured scenes on the entire west coast of Vancouver Island.

During peak summer months, the springs can be fairly crowded during the daytime. To truly enjoy this location, figure out a way to stay overnight in the area. There is a private campground at the trailhead (p. 236) and some basic accommodation is also available in Hot Springs Cove village (p. 236) across the harbour from the trailhead. A heritage marine vessel, **The InnChanter**, is moored at the trailhead's dock, providing bed and breakfast accommodation (p. 236).

Departures from Tofino to Hot Springs Cove are in the morning and early afternoon. The hot springs are less accessible by boat from November-February, but some charter companies do remain open year round. The hot springs can be reached year round by float plane, weather permitting. Prices for trips to Hot Springs Cove vary by vessel type, trip length and services offered.

Contact a charter company or tour operator for current prices and travel conditions.

The whale and bear watching companies listed above all offer tours to the hot springs. See page 236 for more information about accommodation and camping near the hot springs trailhead.

TOFINO GUIDE

BIRDWATCHING

Clayoquot Sound is situated on one of the major flyways for migrating birds on the West Coast. Of the estimated 150 species of resident birds in Clayoquot Sound, you might see black oystercatchers, killdeers, western sandpipers, snow geese, black-bellied plovers and common snipes. The critical habitat of the Tofino mudflats, located between the peninsula and Meares Island, is a 21-square kilometre Wildlife Management Area.

The Tofino Mudflats

Your first stop as a birdwatcher should be here, a splendid muddy haven for birds and birders. This estuarine system is alive with a vast diversity of species, from shorebirds to waterfowl to waders. The importance of the Tofino Mudflats as a migratory stopover is recognized by Birdlife International, who designated the area one of Canada's 325 Important Bird Areas.

Great blue herons and bald eagles are commonly sighted year round, particularly on or near the mudflats, but **the very best time for birdwatchers to visit the mudflats is late April through early May**. Tens of thousands of shorebirds utilize the extensive mudflats and beaches in the area as a vital feeding and resting ground. Greater yellowlegs, whimbrels, dunlins, common snipes and dowitchers are all common sights in the spring. Adding to the excitement of the mudflats in spring is the abundance of western sandpipers, least sandpipers and sanderlings. The massive flocks of these birds twisting and turning above Tofino's inlets and beaches present astonishing aerial displays.

The shorebirds return in the fall, but their arrivals are staggered over many weeks, therefore less dramatic than their sudden spring convergence. Autumn's excitement begins in October with a cacophony of honking overhead from thousands of migrating Canada geese. Watch also for the majestic white trumpeter swans, stopping by briefly in the late fall to dabble in protected inlets at high tide.

The winter is waterfowl season at the mudflats. Tens of thousands of ducks arrive here each winter to take advantage of the relatively protected waters and the abundance of food. Buffleheads, northern pintails, white-winged scoters and green-winged teals are commonly sighted species.

A Meares Island tour (p. 96) will provide a partial view of this area, but the best way to view this highly diverse ecosystem is by sea kayak (p. 156) at low tide. Birdwatching at the mudflats is possible from land, but access is limited. The most accessible land-based public viewing area is at the end of Sharp Road (map, p. 115). Another good access point is the waterfront of the Tofino Botanical Gardens (admission fee required, p. 207).

Pelagic Birdwatching

Birds that inhabit the open ocean are referred to as pelagic, and our area of the Pacific Ocean is home to many species of pelagic birds that are rarely, if ever, seen on shore. These species are highly sought-after by many birders looking for rare birds to add to their life lists. If you head out to sea some 50 km offshore from Tofino, you enter the territory of south polar skuas, pomarine and parasitic jaegers, pink-footed and sooty shearwaters and northern fulmars. It is difficult to arrange a pelagic birding tour because the weather must cooperate with the timing of the trip. High seas are common offshore, and birdwatching is not possible in these conditions. Fall is the most common time to try to get offshore for a birding trip. If you are interested in coordinating a tour, contact **Just Birding** (below) to see if the stars might align in your favour. Luckily, some pelagic bird species stay a little closer to shore. Seabirds that you might see on a whale watching tour include marbled murrelets, tufted puffins, rhinoceros auklets, pigeon guillemots and common murres. These species are all spotted year round in Clayoquot Sound.

Adrian Dorst
250-725-1243, www.adriandorst.com
Bird watching tours and guidance from a celebrated nature photographer and local bird expert.

Just Birding
Guided birding trips by land, canoe or sea.
1260 Pacific Rim Highway, 250-725-8018, www.justbirding.com

TOFINO GUIDE

CULTURAL TOURS

Take the opportunity to paddle with a Nuu-chah-nulth First Nations guide aboard a 34 foot ocean-going canoe. You'll learn about First Nations Culture and the environment in which it flourished. Tours vary from an Islands Paddle to a salmon BBQ at a traditional Tla-o-qui-aht village site, but a sure bet is a paddle to Meares Island followed by a guided hike on the short but awe-inspiring Big Tree Trail (p. 162). One of the many fascinating stories your Tla-o-qui-aht guide tells is about the western red cedar. This **Tree of Life**, as it was known to the Nuu-chah-nulth, provided for people in innumerable ways: parts were crafted into hats, mats, houses, baskets, blankets, clothing... and the canoe you will paddle is carved out of a single tree – most likely by a blood-relative of your guide.

Tla-ook Cultural Adventures
877-942-2663 or 250-725-2656, www.tlaook.com

SCENIC BOAT CHARTERS

Sit back in comfort, motoring past kayakers and canoeists, and watch the ever-changing landscape and seascape of Clayoquot Sound. Many of these scenic motorboat cruises encourage you to bring your own picnic and most offer sunset cruising. This is an excellent option for families or larger groups wanting to move at a calm pace through protected waters.

Browning Pass Charters
250-725-2618, www.browningpass.com

Clayoquot Connections Tours
250-726-8789, www.island.net/~dkay

Tofino Water Taxi
250-725-5485 or 877-726-5485, www.tofinowatertaxi.com

SCENIC FLIGHTS

Two local airline companies offer scenic flights aboard small float planes for folks who like to see things from a different vantage point. The standard scenic flight takes passengers over the Mariner Mountain glacier. The glacier on Mariner is visible from Tofino as you look north towards the mountains over the inlet waters. Seen from the air, the view of this glacier is unparalleled. This trip can be done in as little as 20 minutes, but with a little extra time and some luck you might catch sight of whales from the air. Whale watching from a small plane is the best way to comprehend the truly immense size of these animals.

Atleo Air
50 Wingen Lane, 866-662-8536 or 250-725-2205,
www.atleoair.com

Tofino Air
50 First Street, 866-486-3247 or 250-725-4454, www.tofinoair.ca

TOFINO GUIDE

SEA KAYAKING

Most of the waters of Clayoquot Sound are protected from the open ocean by islands and fjords, offering exciting opportunities to enjoy the art of kayaking. Outings are led by professional guides and offer safe and informative journeys. No experience or special gear is required when you take a trip with qualified guides. Tour companies welcome folks of all ages and moderate physical fitness.

One of the most popular sea kayak tours includes a short, guided hike on the Big Tree Trail on Meares Island (p 162). The trail is home to some of the largest western red cedars on the planet and is well worth the trip.

If you are not interested in a kayak tour you can rent a kayak at **Tofino Sea Kayaking** or bring your own boat. **Make sure you are prepared for Clayoquot Sound's dangerous waters before venturing out on your own** (p. 154). For more information about exploring the waters of Clayoquot Sound in your own boat, see page 153.

Black Bear Kayaking
634 Campbell Street at Weigh West Marine Resort, 250-725-3277, www.blackbearkayak.com

Paddle West Kayaking
606 Campbell Street, 800-667-9913 or 250-725-3919, www.paddlewestkayaking.com

Remote Passages
51 Wharf Street, 800-666-9833 or 250-725-3330, www.remotepassages.com

Tofino Sea Kayaking
320 Main Street, 800-863-4664 or 250-725-4222, www.tofino-kayaking.com

SPORT FISHING

You can choose from a variety of fishing charter options. The larger companies are able to host single or multiple boat groups and the smaller companies tend to run with one vessel - everything from a 17 foot open inshore craft for fly fishing or light tackle, to a 30-plus foot covered cruiser for offshore excursions. Salmon fishing in Clayoquot Sound mostly focuses on two different species: coho (or silver) salmon and chinook (or king) salmon. Both species can be caught in the ocean's near-shore and offshore waters on a wide variety of gear. The offshore waters also have excellent halibut fishing.

Remote freshwater fishing options are available for the adventurous types. Float planes provide anglers access to streams and lakes in pristine settings within Clayoquot Sound. Steelhead, rainbow and cutthroat trout inhabit these waters. When fish are caught on the remote freshwater excursions they are carefully released. Bring your camera to help capture the memories.

If you are planning to go fishing without a guide, Clayoquot Sound is well-suited for your excursion. Tofino has a full service fly and tackle shop, plenty of marine services and lots of local advice. Use extra caution and common sense if you plan any boating in the area. See **Getting off the Peninsula** (p. 153) for more information about exploring Clayoquot Sound's waters.

It is illegal to fish anywhere without a fishing license. Double check that your guide service has taken care of this, or purchase your own if you are fishing without a guide. See page 185 to find a store that sells licenses.

Biggar Fish Charters
120 Fourth Street at Shorewind Gallery, 800-307-0277 or 250-726-8987, www.biggarfish.com

Braedy Mack Fishing Charters
250-726-8499, www.braedymack.com

TOFINO GUIDE

Chinook Charters
331 Main Street, 250-726-5221, www.chinookcharters.com

Clayoquot Ventures Guide Service
561 Campbell Street, 888-534-7422 or 250-725-2700,
www.tofinofishing.com

Hymax Charters
700 Industrial Way, 250-266-0147, www.hymaxcharters.com

Ospray Charters
450 Neill Street, 888-286-3466 or 250-725-2133,
www.ospray.com

Sport Fishing with Chris Barker
341 Olsen Road, 250-725-8200, www.tofinosportfishing.com

Tofino Fish Guides
877-537-6444 or 250-266-0587

Tofinotyee
326B Peterson Drive, 250-522-0060 or 250-725-1239
www.tofinotyee.com

Weigh West Marine Resort
634 Campbell Street, 800-665-8922 or 250-725-3277,
www.weighwest.com

SCUBA DIVING

The West Coast is known as the Graveyard of the Pacific and Clayoquot Sound has its share of undersea wrecks. The clear ocean waters provide exploration challenges for SCUBA divers from all over the world. Despite the region's extensive underwater exploration, the elusive wreck of the *Tonquin* has yet to be found. This famous vessel, purportedly within 5 kilometres of Tofino, is believed to be loaded with nineteenth century artefacts (p. 62).

Ocean Planet Adventures
465 Campbell Street, 888.725.2220 or 250-725-2221,
www.oceanplanetadventures.com

Offers diving tours, lessons and PADI certification courses. They also offer snorkelling tours if you prefer powering yourself with your own lungs.

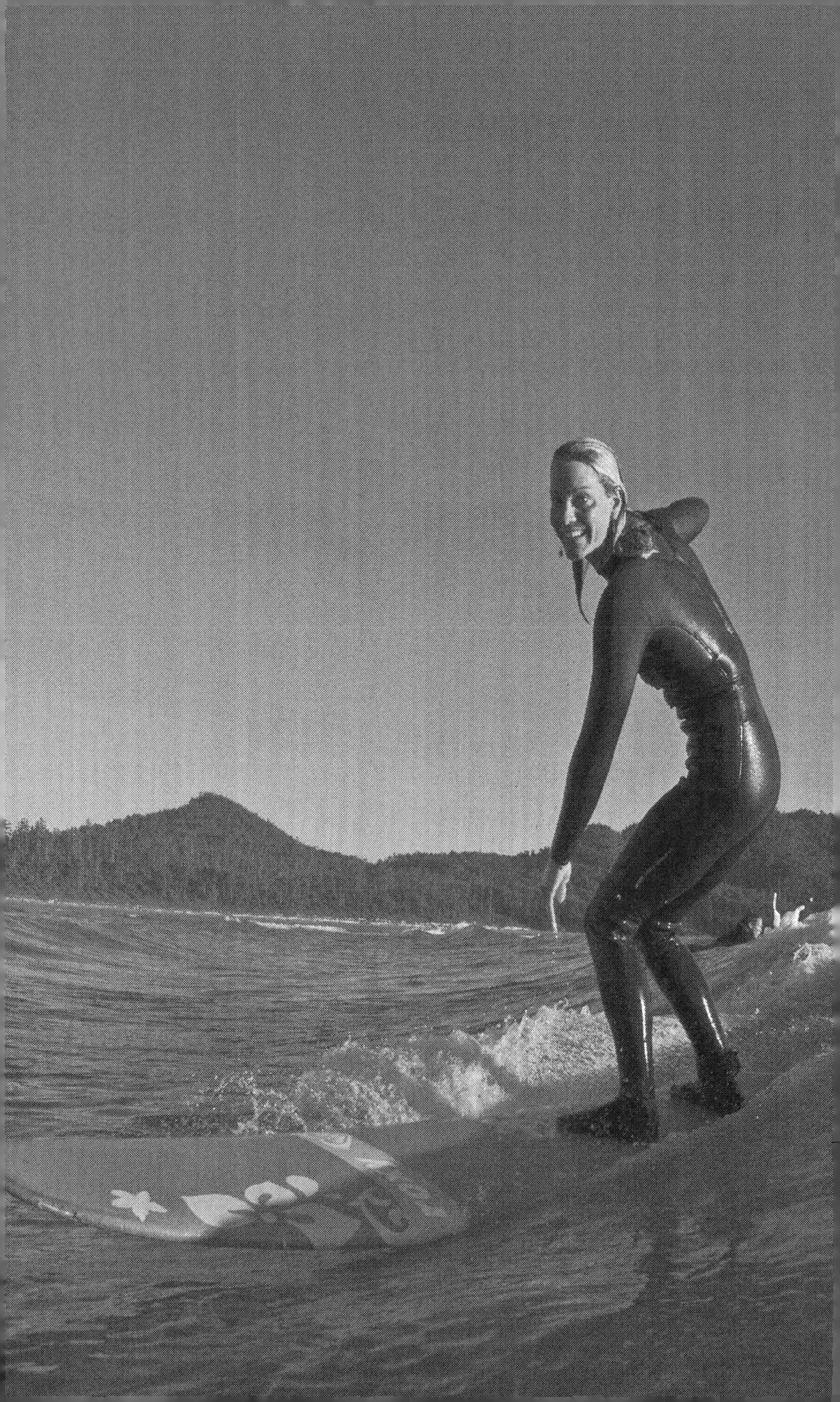

SURFING

The Surfing Capital of Canada
Where Do I Start?
Chesterman Beach Surfing
Cox Bay Surfing
Long Beach Surfing
Surf Shops and Surfing Gear Rentals
Surfing Lessons

TOFINO GUIDE

THE SURFING CAPITAL OF CANADA

In the 1960s the new road to Tofino attracted many newcomers, most of them drawn to the dramatic beaches and wilderness, and some to the lively beach-dwelling subculture that emerged here in the late 60s. Some of these folks had surfed before, and began to test the waters here. In the summer of 1968, a small surf school operated on Long Beach and by the mid-70s Tofino was becoming known as a place where small groups of people were surfing regularly during the spring and summer months.

From this scrappy beginning, the Tofino surfing scene has grown into a multi-million dollar industry, and a few of the proprietors of local surfing businesses are offspring of the early surf explorers. Now you'll find resorts with surf packages, surf shops, surf schools, week-long surf camps and numerous equipment rental venues. Wetsuit technology has progressed to the point where serious surfers will spend many comfortable hours in the water year round, taking full advantage of the large and consistent winter swells.

In November of 2009, the O'Neil Coldwater Classic surfing competition came to Tofino. By staging this event here, the professional surfing world officially recognized the world class level of Tofino's many beach breaks and joined forces with our relaxed Canadian surfing culture. While there have been numerous surfing competitions on the beaches of Tofino over the years, this was the first official World Qualifying Series event in Canadian water. The healthy pride of local residents knew no bounds when one of our own, local wildcard entry Peter Devries, won the top $20,000 cash prize. As if to honour this occasion, Tofino's mayor and council officially declared Tofino the **Surfing Capital of Canada** that same month.

WHERE DO I START?

If you are new to surfing we recommend you take a surf lesson from one of the surf schools and rent gear from a local company.

If you choose not to take a lesson, at least ask your surf shop about the best beach for beginners, given the current wind and swell conditions. See page 106 for listings of surf schools, shops and rental companies.

The Internet can be a good place to start to learn what beach might be appropriate for you. **MagicSeaweed.com** provides a good overview of the current wind and swell conditions (our area is listed as Vancouver Island North). You'll need to know which way the different beaches are oriented in order to match MagicSeaweed's data to Tofino's beaches. In the simplest terms, surfers look for a swell heading toward the direction a beach faces and the wind direction to be opposing the beach's facing direction ('offshore'). So a south-facing beach is best on a swell from the south and winds from the north.

Below we provide the rock-bottom basics about surfing at four different beaches below.

CHESTERMAN BEACH SURFING

Chesterman Beach is Canada's most popular beach for folks learning how to surf. **In 2010, *Outside Magazine* declared Chesterman "one of the best beginner breaks in North America."**

Located about 8 minutes drive from central Tofino, with ample parking, this is the most accessible beach of all. There are two parts to Chesterman's: South and North.

South Chesterman beach faces roughly south, so it is a good place to surf if there is a south swell and a northwest wind (the wind rarely arrives from due north). Access to this part of the beach is just off Pacific Rim Highway on Chesterman Beach Road. There is a composting toilet facility in the parking lot.

North Chesterman beach faces roughly west, so is a good place to surf if the swell direction is west or northwest and the wind

TOFINO GUIDE

direction is southeast (the wind rarely arrives from due east). Access to North Chesterman is through a large parking lot on Lynn Road. Currently there is no toilet facility here, although one is planned to be completed before summer 2011.

Some folks refer to 'Middle' Chesterman as a geographic reference. This is accessed at the southern curve of Chesterman Beach Road and is the point where the sandspit (technically a 'tombolo') reaches out to Frank Island. This is a good place to get a strategic sense of the surfing conditions at South and North Chesterman.

North Chesterman Webcam
www.surfcam.ca

COX BAY SURFING

Cox Bay is one of the most consistent surfing beaches in the summer months. The beach faces west and picks up smaller summer swells that often elude North Chesterman's. Try this beach if the swell is small and from the west or northwest. Ideally you'll want a southeast wind or no wind, but unfortunately both of these winds are rare in the summer.

The first access to Cox Bay is just south of the **Cox Bay Visitor Centre**: turn down Maltby Road and then left at the end of the short road into a parking lot. From the parking lot, go through the yellow gate down a short gravel trail through the forest to the beach. There is a composting toilet at the beach end of this trail.

The second access to Cox Bay is at **Cox Bay Beach Resort** across the road from the Cox Bay Visitor Centre. Park in the lot labelled public parking and walk the short boardwalk trail to the beach. There are bathroom and shower facilities at the parking lot.

Pacific Sands Resort and **Long Beach Lodge** have webcams on their roofs overlooking Cox Bay. These cameras can be a good way to check the surf from your hotel room or your mobile device. Sneaking through the grounds of Pacific Sands Beach Resort or Long Beach Lodge to check the surf is frowned upon. Please respect their private property.

Cox Bay Webcams
www.westcoastaquatic.ca/webcam.htm
www.pacificsands.com/WebCam.html

LONG BEACH SURFING

Long Beach, located in Pacific Rim National Park, is about a twenty-five minute drive from Tofino. Long Beach is without doubt Tofino's (and arguably Canada's) most famous beach. Along its 16 km of sand, you will find waves suited to all levels of surfing. As you approach from Tofino, the first parking lot at Long Beach is signed **Incinerator Rock**. This location is usually full of surfers, surfing talk, and of course the latest in surfing fashion. In the summer months it's best to park in the second parking lot, signed Long Beach. Please read the signs posted at both parking lots about dangerous currents.

Most of Long Beach faces southwest, so you'll do best here on a southwest swell with a northwest wind. There are bathroom and shower facilities at both of Long Beach's access points.

TOFINO GUIDE

SURF SHOPS AND SURFING GEAR RENTALS

Live to Surf
1180 Pacific Rim Highway, 250-725-4464, www.livetosurf.com
Rents all the gear you need for surfing or boogie boarding. Clothes, skateboards, surfboards and everything to do with surfing is available at their very large surf shop.

Long Beach Surf Shop
630 Campbell Street, 250-725-3800, www.longbeachsurfshop.com
Rents all the gear you need for surfing and boogie boarding. Big selection of skateboards, surfboards, wetsuits and surf styles, in a fun atmosphere. Also sells music on vinyl and CD.

Pacific Surf School
430 Campbell Street, 250-725-2155 or 888-777-9961,
www.pacificsurfschool.com
Pacific Surf School rents all the surfing or boogie boarding gear you need, even if you choose not to take a lesson with them.

Storm Surf Shop
444 Campbell Street, 250-725-3344, www.stormcanada.ca
Large selection of surfboards, skate boards, wetsuits and accessories for sale. Known for "in vogue" clothing and surf styles, this busy shop is Tofino's trend setter.

Surf Sister Surf School
625 Campbell Street, 250-725-4456 or 877-724-7873,
www.surfsister.com
Fully stocked store specializing in surf styles for women.

SURFING LESSONS

Bruhwiler Surf School
311 Olsen Road, 250-726-5481, www.bruhwilersurf.com
Lessons and camps for men and women

Pacific Surf School
430 Campbell Street, 250-725-2155 or 888-777-9961,
www.pacificsurfschool.com
Lessons and camps for men and women

Surf Sister Surf School
625 Campbell Street, 250-725-4456 or 877-724-7873,
www.surfsister.com
Lessons and camps for men and women

Tofino Surf School
566 Campbell Street, 250-725-2711, www. tofinosurfschool.ca
Lessons for men and women

Westside Surf School
1180 Pacific Rim Highway (Live to Surf parking lot), 250-725-2404,
www.westsidesurfschool.com
Lessons and camps for men and women

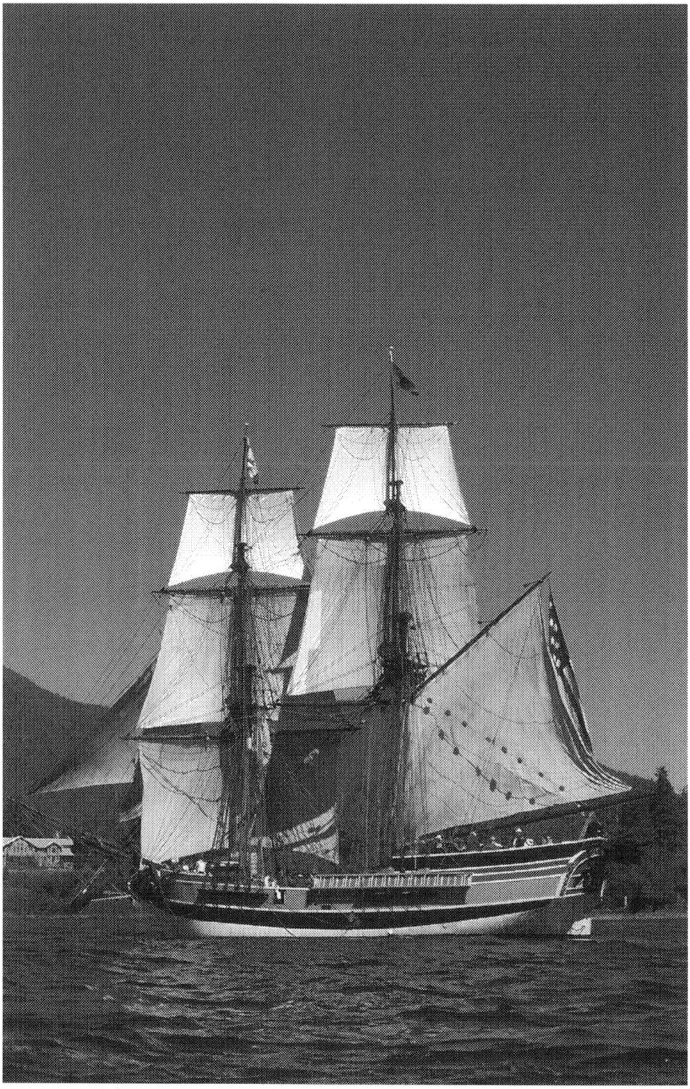

MAPS

Getting Here

*Pacific Rim National Park Reserve
(showing hikes)*

District of Tofino (showing beaches)

Downtown Tofino

Cape Scott

Brooks Peninsula

Kyuquot

VANCOUVER ISLAND

Nootka Island

PACIFIC OCEAN

Estevan Point

CLAYOQUOT SOUND

TOFINO

Ucluelet

0   100 Kilometres
0   50 Miles

Approximate Driving Times to Tofino*

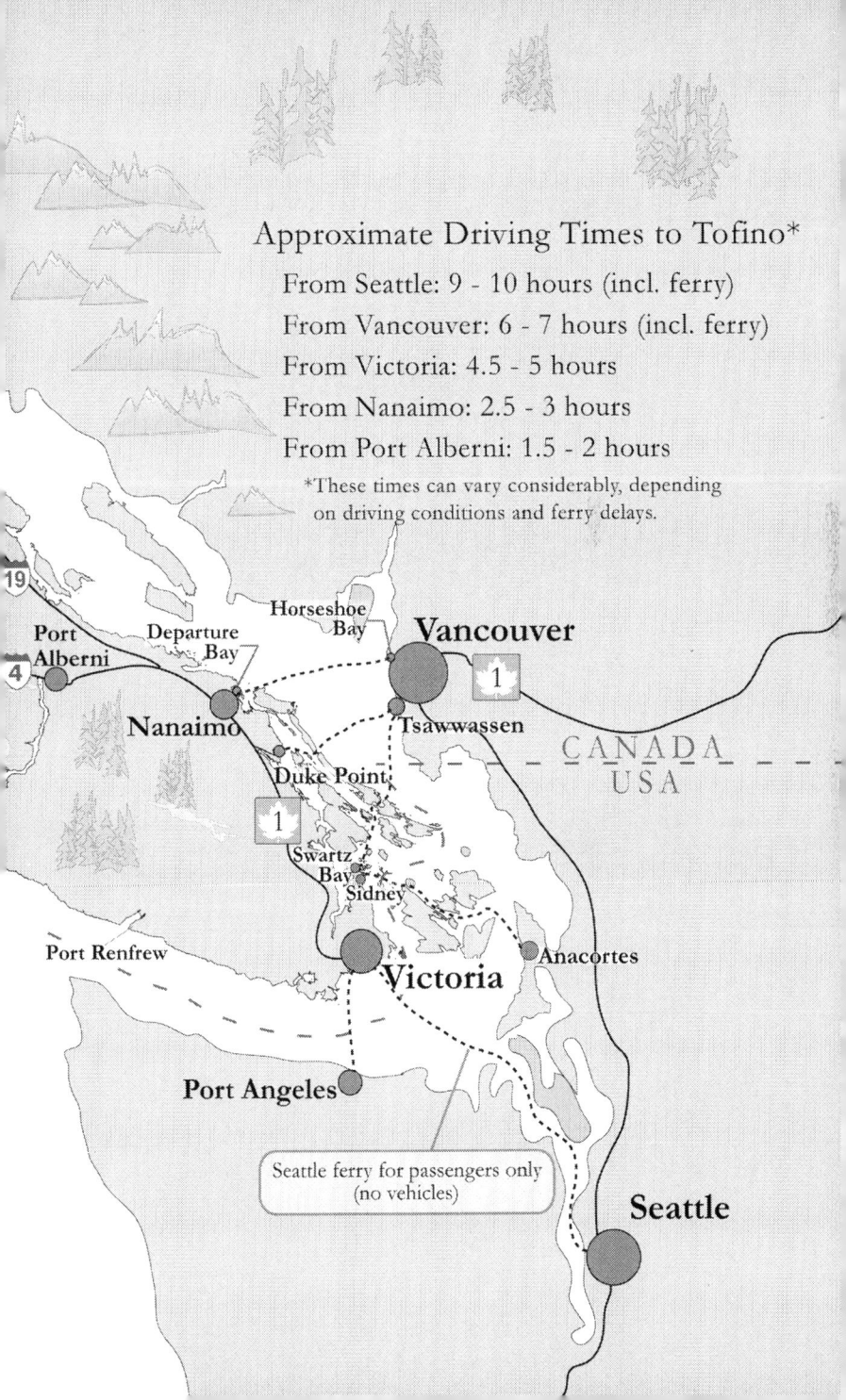

From Seattle: 9 - 10 hours (incl. ferry)
From Vancouver: 6 - 7 hours (incl. ferry)
From Victoria: 4.5 - 5 hours
From Nanaimo: 2.5 - 3 hours
From Port Alberni: 1.5 - 2 hours

*These times can vary considerably, depending on driving conditions and ferry delays.

Seattle ferry for passengers only (no vehicles)

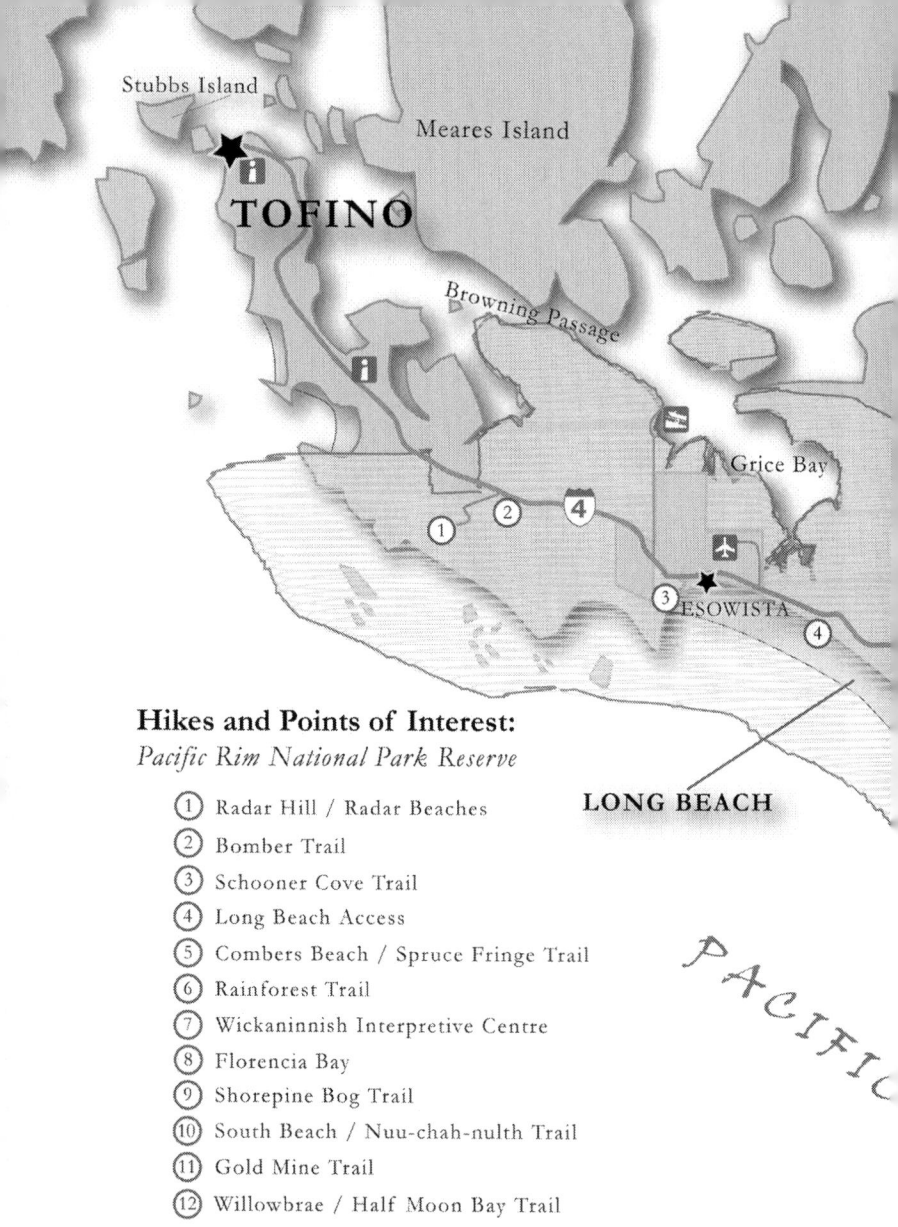

Hikes and Points of Interest:
Pacific Rim National Park Reserve

1. Radar Hill / Radar Beaches
2. Bomber Trail
3. Schooner Cove Trail
4. Long Beach Access
5. Combers Beach / Spruce Fringe Trail
6. Rainforest Trail
7. Wickaninnish Interpretive Centre
8. Florencia Bay
9. Shorepine Bog Trail
10. South Beach / Nuu-chah-nulth Trail
11. Gold Mine Trail
12. Willowbrae / Half Moon Bay Trail

- Pacific Rim National Park Reserve
- Vistor Information Centre
- Tofino Airport
- Grice Bay Boat Launch

Tofino Inlet

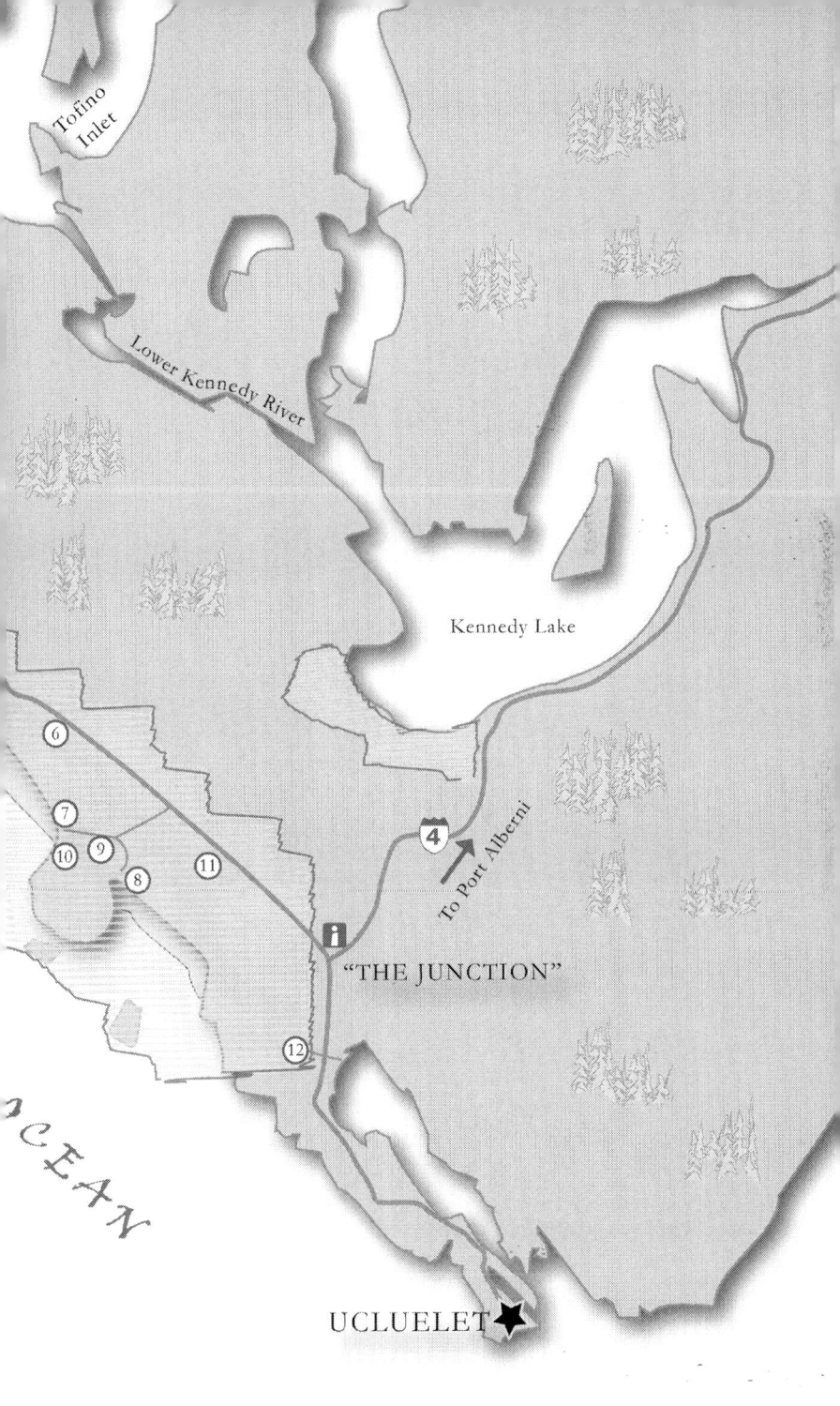

Lower Kennedy River

Kennedy Lake

⑥
⑦
⑩ ⑨
⑧ ⑪

④ To Port Alberni

"THE JUNCTION"

⑫

OCEAN

UCLUELET ★

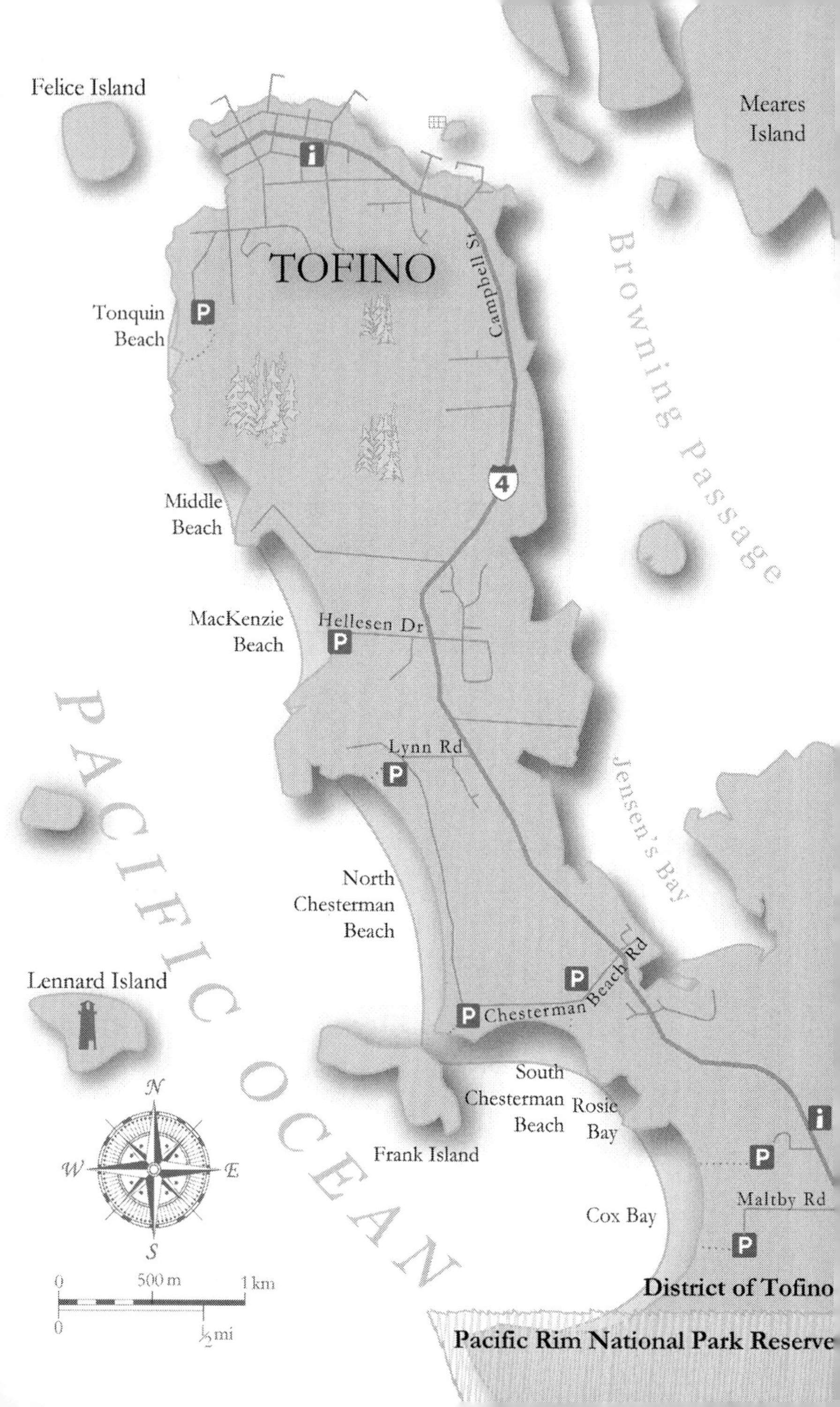
Felice Island
Meares Island
TOFINO
Campbell St
Browning Passage
Tonquin Beach
4
Middle Beach
MacKenzie Beach
Hellesen Dr
Lynn Rd
Jensen's Bay
PACIFIC OCEAN
North Chesterman Beach
Lennard Island
Chesterman Beach Rd
South Chesterman Beach
Rosie Bay
Frank Island
Cox Bay
Maltby Rd
N
S
W
E
0
500 m
1 km
½ mi
District of Tofino
Pacific Rim National Park Reserve

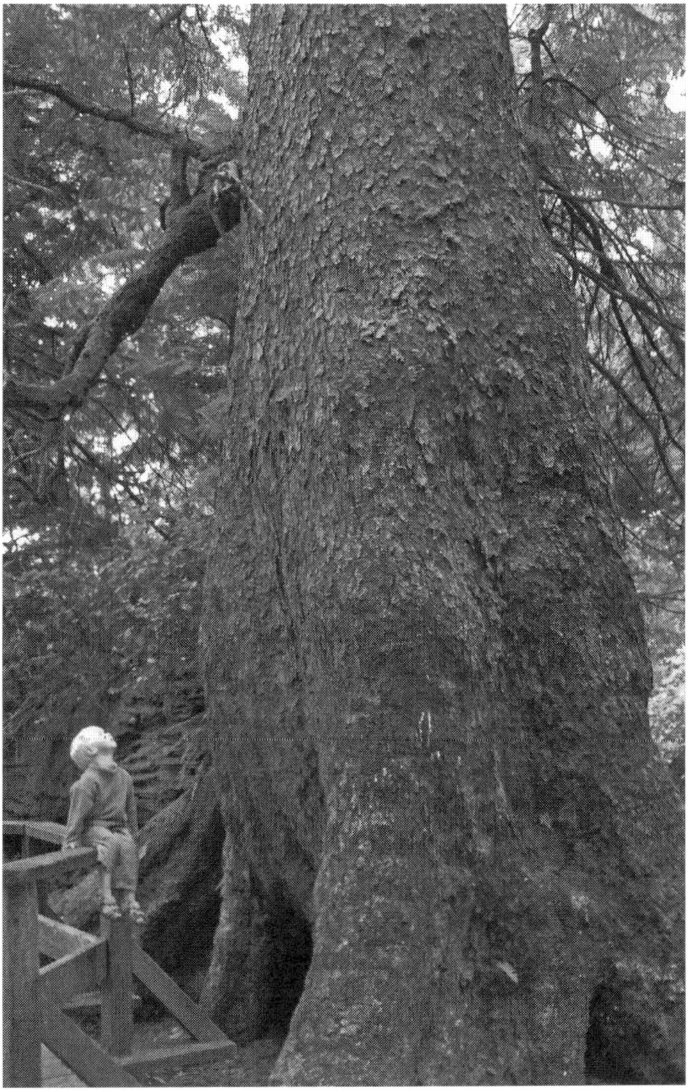

First Street Dock

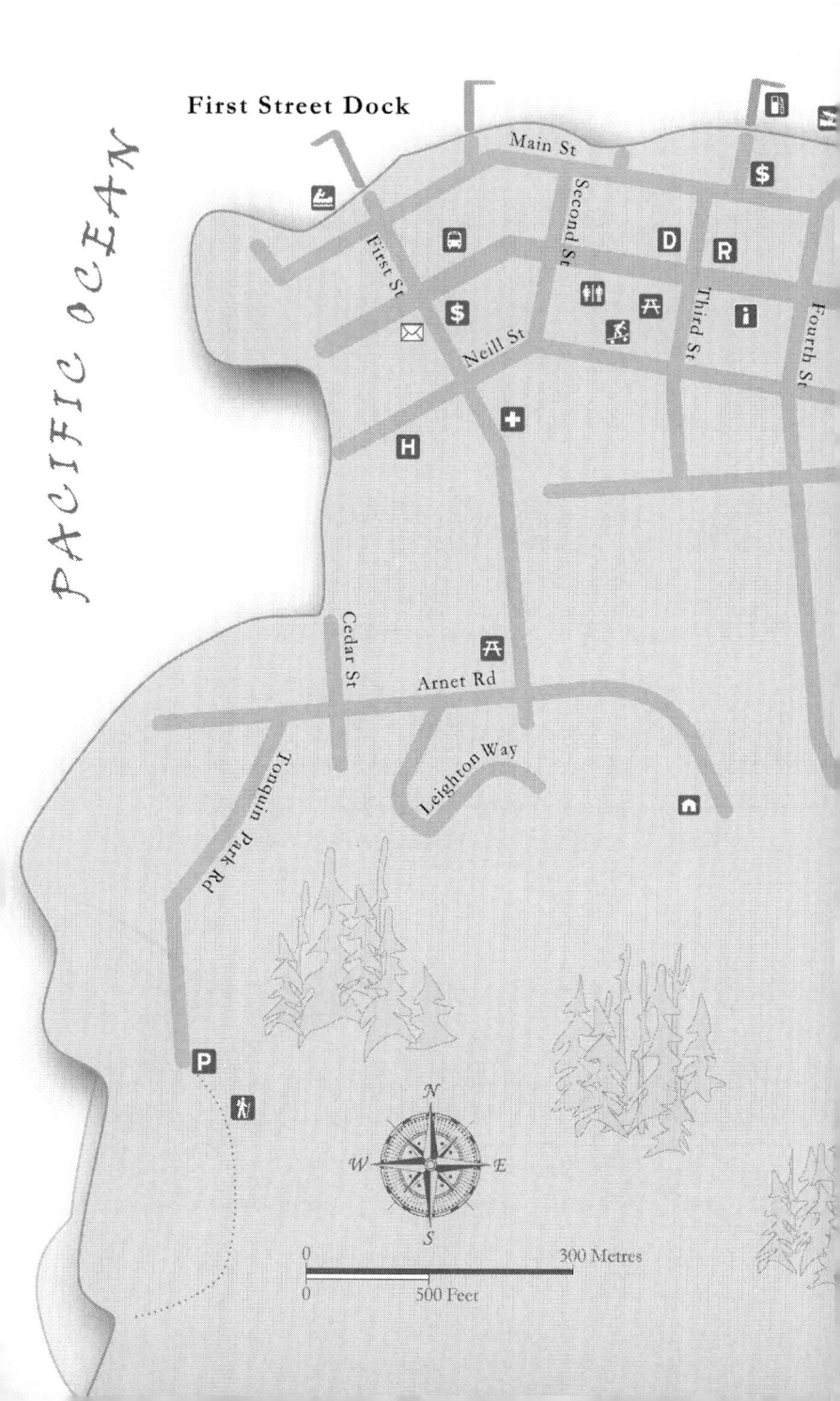

Fourth Street Dock

Strawberry Island

Campbell St

Gibson St

Crab Dock

Pfeiffer Cr

Lone Cone St

Neilson Pl

Minto Pl

Pacific Rim Hwy

TOFINO

- H Hospital
- Medical Clinic
- S Bank
- Post Office
- R RCMP (Police)
- Tofino Bus
- i Visitor Information
- Public Restroom
- Tonquin Beach Trail
- D District of Tofino Office
- Tofino Community Hall
- Kayak & Canoe Launch
- Fuel Dock
- Boat Launch
- Park with Children's Play Area
- Skateboard, Basketball, Tennis

(4)

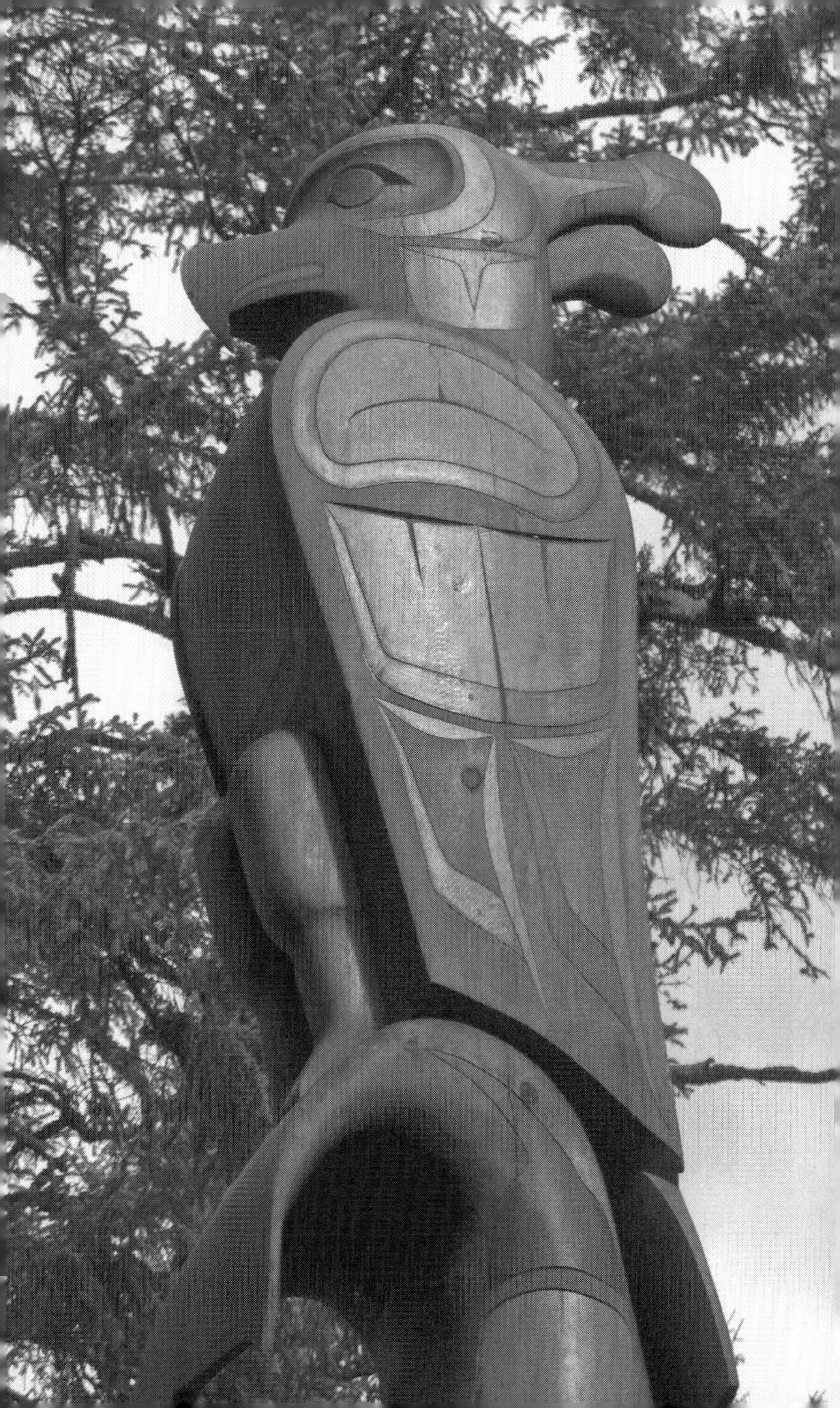

HIKING IN PACIFIC RIM NATIONAL PARK RESERVE

Don't make us rescue you – Hiking Safety Tips
Encounters with Bears, Cougars or Wolves

Radar Beaches (p. 123)

Radar Hill View Point (p. 125)

Bomber Trail (p. 126)

Schooner Cove Trail (p. 128)

Long Beach (p. 130)

Spruce Fringe Trail (p. 132)

Combers Beach (p. 133)

Rain Forest Trail, Loops A & B (p. 135)

Florencia Bay Beach
(also called Wreck Bay) (p. 138)

Shorepine Bog Trail (p. 140)

South Beach Trail (p. 142)

Nuu-chah-nulth Trail (p. 144)

Gold Mine Trail (p. 146)

Willowbrae Trail (p. 149)

Half Moon Bay Trail (p. 150)

TOFINO GUIDE

DON'T MAKE US RESCUE YOU – HIKING SAFETY TIPS

Hiking in the Tofino area and the Pacific Rim National Park Reserve is not overtly dangerous, but you and your hiking party should keep a few important safety tips at the front of your minds:

- **Always stay on the trail**: it is easy to lose your sense of direction in the forest

- It gets dark quickly during most of the year here and daylight fades even more quickly in the forest. Carry a headlamp with spare batteries.

- **Keep a close eye on kids** while hiking on the beaches and in the forest. It is extremely rare, but there are records of cougars stalking children in coastal British Columbia.

- Boardwalks can become very slippery. Use additional caution on boardwalks in wet weather.

- **Be aware of the times that tides shift**. Knowing this information will help you make intelligent decisions when hiking along the beach.

- **Always let someone know where you are going** and when you expect to be back. Remember to check with your contact on your return.

- Carrying a cellular phone is a good idea, but **do not rely on your cellular phone** for communication, as reception is patchy in areas of Pacific Rim National Park.

- GPS works in most areas of the park but **satellite communication is unreliable under the temperate rainforest's thick canopy**.

- Carry snacks, water, sunscreen, sunhat, raingear and any other equipment appropriate to the conditions in a small backpack.

ENCOUNTERS WITH BEARS, COUGARS OR WOLVES

You may come across these animals anywhere in the area. Know what to do.

Consult the park brochures "You Are in Wolf and Cougar Country" and "You are in Black Bear Country". The brochures are available at the Visitor Centres (p. 25), Green Point Campground (p. 237), and the Wickaninnish Interpretive Centre (p. 79).

Groups of people are safer than lone hikers.

Remember to **keep your distance** from these animals. The more distance between you and the animal, the safer it is for you and the animal. **"Space is Safe"**.

If a wolf, cougar or bear does not walk away from your group, scare it away by shouting and waving your arms. If this does not work, throw rocks or sticks at the animal. The group should act together to scare the animal.

If you have a dog, the best way to ensure its safety is to **keep it on a leash**. In the Pacific Rim National Park Reserve this is required by law.

Check information centres and **watch for signs posting current wildlife sightings**.

To find out more about predators and their interactions with people in this region **read the *WildCoast Primer: Learning to Live with Large Carnivores***. This helpful resource is available online: www.clayoquotbiosphere.org/wildcoast.

Please **report wolf and cougar sightings in Pacific Rim National Park Reserve to Parks Canada staff** at 250-726-7165. For wolf and cougar sightings outside the park, call 1-877-952-7277.

TOFINO GUIDE

Trailhead Locations

This section of our guide is presented in geographic order. We start at the northern edge of the Pacific Rim National Park Reserve and continue along the highway heading southwest along Highway 4 to cover all of the hikes in the Pacific Rim National Park Reserve.

RADAR BEACHES

Not on the park map, this is a challenging unofficial route leading to three small, secluded beaches. Be warned, **many people have become lost on this route** putting their personal safety at risk and resulting in costly searches. Carry a cell phone and a headlamp, let someone know where you are going, when you expect to be back and remember to notify this person when you return. This route is not maintained but the rewards can be worth the trek.

Drive 10.5 km south of Tofino, turn right at the Radar Hill sign. Follow the road up. Be aware that there are hidden bumps in this paved road. Park in the farthest, western-most parking area. Go to the clearing in the trees, across the parking lot from the small toilet facility. Facing the ocean, look to the south (left) about 10 metres and you will see the beginning of a narrow route. This is the start of the route to the Radar Beaches. Make sure you have packed a lunch and plenty of drinking water because you will want to rest, explore and restore your energy once you reach the bottom. The route basically follows a creek (and the route itself sometimes seems like a creek in wet weather) down the side of the mountain. **This is not a winter hike**.

At the beginning, the route descends steeply, at times almost a vertical drop. Within 15 minutes you will be scaling down a 10 metre drop, using tree roots as grips and footholds. The route demands agility and you are sure to become dirty or muddy so dress appropriately. After about 20 minutes of descent the route continues more gradually, and you will find you are walking over or through large puddles, balancing on logs to cross the streams, and hopping up on stumps or fallen logs to keep from getting soaked.

The second time that you cross a log over a stream, about 40 minutes into the hike, you are close to the end of the route and should hear the ocean in the near distance. When you finally begin to emerge from the forest, you will ascend a short rise from the stream bed and emerge onto a sand beach in front of you.

TOFINO GUIDE

This first beach, the largest of the three Radar Beaches is about 400 metres long. The northern end of this beach, to your right, is a rocky headland with a small cave that is fun to poke around in. You could continue to walk south (left), either following animal trails through the forest or scrambling over large headlands. If you choose to continue south, a chain of two small beaches await you, making your scramble well worthwhile.

Make sure that you leave yourself plenty of time and daylight to get back to the Radar Hill parking lot well before dark. Remember you will be returning uphill, and that **you lose daylight very quickly in the forest**, especially in the late summer and fall months. Remember also to watch the tides on this hike.

Hiking Time
About 1 hour going down, longer, about 1.5 hours coming back up. This does not include the explorations to the south. Add 1.5 hours to explore the three southern beaches.

Length
1 km steep descent to the beach, then return

Location
10.5 km south of Tofino, turn right at the Radar Hill sign. Follow the road up. Be aware that there are hidden bumps in this paved road.

Difficulty
Difficult. Expect to get muddy, sweaty, possibly wet. Wear sturdy shoes or hiking boots.

Please Remember
The Long Beach Unit of the park has one campground, Green Point (p. 237), which has both drive-in and walk-in campsites. **There is no camping on Radar Beaches.**

Dogs are required to be on-leash in the National Park at all times.

RADAR HILL VIEW POINT

Go to the Radar Hill turnoff as described above. Stop immediately to your right and purchase your Park Pass if you do not already have one. Continue in your vehicle up the hill and park at the first of two parking areas, labelled Kap'yong Memorial. This is where there the trail to the viewing platforms begins. If the Kap'yong parking area is full, continue 35 metres to the end of the road and park in the second parking area.

To reach the viewing platforms, find the wide concrete path beginning at the interpretive sign and Kap'yong Memorial. The memorial commemorates a fierce battle in 1951 during the Korean War.

Take a moment to read the interpretive sign describing the circumstances that led to building this former radar station in 1954. Now begin ascending the short, wheelchair accessible path leading up to the summit of Radar Hill.

Each of the four viewing areas has an impressive view. Our favourite is the first platform on your left that looks north over Clayoquot Sound including Meares, Flores, and Vargas Islands. Amazingly, you cannot see any evidence of Tofino or of any logging from this location. **This view has not been altered in thousands of years.** At sundown this spot turns from spectacular to magical. It is high on our **Pacific Rim National Park Reserve Top Ten list** (p. 82).

Length
Very short uphill walk (under 5 minutes) to each viewing area then return.

Location
10.5 km south of Tofino, turn right at the Radar Hill sign. Follow the road up. **Be aware that there are hidden bumps in this paved road that are potentially damaging to your vehicle if you drive over 20 km per hour.**

Difficulty
Easy: Wheelchair accessible.

BOMBER TRAIL

The Park maps do not to show this route, but we think the site of this 1945 plane crash is well worth a visit. That said, **HEED THIS WARNING**: The route, while moderately easy can be difficult to follow and is usually muddy. A number of animal trails criss-cross the route and hikers often become confused. A yellow rope has been strung tree-to-tree through the worst and most confusing portion of the route, and there are a number of metal marker posts with reflective tape marking the way. Despite these helpful way finders, take care to stay on route. **Many hikers have become lost overnight on this route**, necessitating involved searches to locate and assist them.

Do not attempt this route within four hours of sunset. As with the Radar Beaches Route, give yourself plenty of time, carry a headlamp and a cell phone, and let someone know where you are going and when you expect to return. And again, let your contact know when you are back.

The start of the route is not easy to find: 10.5 km south of Tofino, turn right at the Radar Hill sign. Park in the first parking area on your right, about 100 metres off the highway before you go up the big hill. Walk back out to the highway and head south for 500 metres. On the right hand side, you will notice an old road turnoff that disappears through the trees. Hop the ditch and begin walking up the slightly overgrown road leading up the hill. Fairly soon you will come to an abandoned building, apparently some type of machine shop. Opposite this building, you will see an opening in the heavy growth of the forest. A ribbon of surveyor's tape marks this opening. This is the entrance to Bomber Route.

The route descends for a period through dense brush and forest before levelling off. Take your time on this route or you will quickly become confused and lost. Before venturing past any one marker ribbon, look ahead and get a sighting of the next one. They are usually about 20 metres apart. The route gives the general impression of veering to the right, but bear in mind how easy it is to lose your bearings in dense forest, especially when lighting is poor. **Continually check for marker ribbons**.

About 45 minutes after leaving the highway, take note of the remarkably deep-looking circular pond, about 8 metres across. This pond was created by a controlled explosion following the accident. The plane was carrying four depth charges that remained intact on impact, and these explosives were later detonated by members of the Royal Canadian Air Force.

Stay to the left of the pond and you will come across the heritage site marker. The position of the bomber should now be evident just beyond where you are.

Avoid taking any side trails or hiking uphill past the plane. Usually these actions have been the cause of people getting lost. The route is not a loop. You have to hike back out the same way you hiked in.

None of the twelve people on board died in the crash and the pilot – or so the story goes – only suffered a twisted ankle. The skeleton of his plane remains virtually intact despite decades of souvenir hunters who have stripped the wreckage of all but its outer shell.

Hiking Time
50 minutes to an hour one way

Length
2 km one way

Location
11 km south of Tofino, just beyond Radar Hill turnoff

Difficulty
Moderate. Up and down, lots of roots and very wet. Good navigation skills and common sense required.

TOFINO GUIDE

SCHOONER COVE TRAIL

This trail puts you at the northern end of world-renowned **Long Beach**. To reach the start of the trail, as you are heading away from Tofino, turn right off the highway at the Schooner sign, about 15 km from the Post Office, and park in the lot.

The trailhead is at the southwestern corner of the parking lot. It begins by winding through a thicket of second growth cedar and hemlock trees. Note when you cross into the true old growth rainforest. You should be able to feel the temperature drop as the light recedes and the trees increase in size.

This is a fairly easy trail to navigate, although you will descend and ascend through a couple of gullies, up and down many sets of stairs and across a small bridge.

As you hike you will pass through an ancient forest of giant cedars and massive Sitka spruce for about 20 minutes. Just before you reach the beach you will make your way through a large stand of salmonberry bushes (*Rubus spectabilis*). It is said that the salmonberry ripen only after the salmon fry have hatched in the early summer. If your timing is right you should try the berries. They are generally pale red or orange in colour, and they resemble raspberries, though they have a softer texture and are less acidic.

Nearing the end of the trail, you will finally begin to hear the surf. Then you descend steeply to the beach, following a steep set of about 60 stairs. Upon arrival at the beach, you can either head to your left and walk south down **Long Beach** or turn right (north) and head to a smaller but more secluded set of beaches.

If you choose to go left (south) you will pass by houses that are part of the **Tla-o-qui-aht First Nation Reserve of Esowista**. The Tla-o-qui-aht people have been summering on this part of the coast for thousands of years. Today, Esowista village is a year round settlement surrounded by National Park on three sides and the Pacific Ocean on the other. Please respect the privacy of the residents here, and do not trespass in the village. See page 37 for more information about the Nuu-chah-nulth First Nations.

If you choose to go north, check out the headlands at the end of the second beach. Walk right out to the reasonably accessible point on these headlands and discover a perfect spot to have lunch, watch the waves, and scan the horizon for sea lions on the rocks, or whales beyond.

Hiking Time
About 50 minutes depending how far you choose to go

Length
1-2 km (one way)

Location
15 km south of the Post Office, turn right at the Schooner Trail turnoff

Difficulty
Moderate. Up and down several gullies and a steep descent of stairs at the end. Boardwalk most of the way.

TOFINO GUIDE

LONG BEACH

Two parking lots access Long Beach. These spots are fairly close to the northern end of the beach.

The more northerly parking lot, at the **Incinerator Rock** sign, is usually full in the summer months, as it has the quickest access to the surf. This parking lot can be hectic with surfers stopping by to check the surf. If you have your heart set on parking here, arrive early and stake your claim. Be prepared for the occasional bare bum as many harmless surfers change here into their wetsuits.

The larger Long Beach parking area is just down the highway another 500 metres south. Turn at the **Long Beach** sign. Here you can almost always find vacant parking spaces and the short trails leading down to the beach are easy to walk and wheelchair accessible. If you are going to the beach to picnic, it is generally not worth fighting for a parking spot at Incinerator Rock. This Long Beach parking area is a lovely spot in itself and the landscaped areas adjacent to the pavement can provide a nice respite from the summer sun. Fewer surfers come here to park, preferring the more immediate beach access at Incinerator Rock.

Now that you have found a parking spot, **get ready for the longest beach hike of your life**. From the beach access at Incinerator Rock you can hike more than 10 km one way, along the open sandy beach. If you are feeling fit, have a partner drop you and a hiking partner off at the **Schooner Cove Trail** (p. 128) and pick you up at the **Wickaninnish Interpretive Centre** (p. 79), about 18 km total. Please note that there is a rocky section about 8 km south of the Long Beach parking areas that separates Long Beach from **Wickaninnish Beach**. It is possible to scramble around these rocks at high tides, but it is much easier and more pleasant to hike around them at a low tide.

Location
16.5 or 17 km south of the Post Office, depending which parking area you choose.

HOW LONG IS LONG BEACH?

According to Parks Canada the official length of Long Beach is 16 km. True, but only if the total distance includes Schooner Cove, Long Beach, Wickaninnish Beach and Combers Beach. Each of these beaches is separated by rocky headlands, but at a very low tide the sand beaches are referred to collectively as Long Beach. The classic stretch of Long Beach between Schooner Cove and the headland at the north end of Wickaninnish Beach is about 6.5 km.

National Park Reserve

TOFINO GUIDE

SPRUCE FRINGE TRAIL

Turn at the **Combers Beach** turnoff and follow the road to the farthest parking lot where you will see the start of the trail. Starting at sea level, this trail leads through several different ecosystems, from heavy undergrowth typically found at the ocean's edge, through the middle of a Sitka spruce grove with trees whose limbs are densely covered in moss, then through a Pacific crab apple (*Malus fusca*) bog, then up a small rise (80 steps) into old growth rainforest where you pass an 800 year old western red cedar. Here you will also pass beneath the best example of a **nurse log** (p. 44) we have ever seen in this region.

An early pioneer homesteaded here, but any trace of the settlement has long since disappeared. Until the 1950s, locals spoke of the wild cattle that once roamed through this forest. These long-horned beasts, including ferocious bulls, were descendants of the original homesteader's herd. Like a few other groups of free-thinking cattle on the West Coast, once they escaped their domestic bounds they survived for generations, wild and free, striking fear into the hearts of anyone who met them.

This well-marked trail has many helpful and informative signs. By the time you reach the end, you should be able to identify the difference between a western red cedar, Sitka spruce, and western hemlock tree.

Hiking Time
40 to 60 minutes

Length
1.5 km (loop)

Location
22.2 km south of the Post Office, turn right at Combers Beach turnoff

Difficulty
Easy: One short climb of about 80 steps, then down.

COMBERS BEACH

At the southern tip of Long Beach, Combers is another access point to that famously long stretch of sand. Usually this is less crowded than the other parking areas.

The destructive force of the surf became dramatically clear here a few years ago. Parks Canada had to relocate this access point and parking lot because much of the previous parking lot was washed away by years of tidal erosion and by a particularly massive storm in December 2006. Near the end of the trail, see if you can spot evidence of this storm, the same one that rocked the entire West Coast and devastated Stanley Park, in downtown Vancouver.

Long Beach curves inward here, to create the deep crescent of Combers Beach. Because of this significant indentation massive accumulations of driftwood gather here. If you time your visit during a winter storm, you will see whole trees swirling like toothpicks in the salty froth. You can pick your way for hours over the countless tons of driftwood piled up here at the winter high tide line.

Be mindful of incoming tides that can narrow this beach, boxing you into the tangled jungle of driftwood very quickly. **NEVER play in or near the water around floating wood**. These pieces of wood, while buoyant, can hit the sand (or each other) unexpectedly in an outgoing surge, crushing anything caught in their way.

This parking area is sometimes closed in the winter months. If it happens to be open on a winter visit, Combers Beach is a perfect place to watch a winter storm from the safety of the forest's edge.

Hiking Time
About 10 minutes

Length
Approx. 1 km one way

TOFINO GUIDE

Location
Watch for the sign Combers Beach on the west side of the highway, 22.2 km south of the Post Office

Difficulty
Easy: Downhill march to beach, then return uphill. It may be awkward to get down to the beach at times – especially outside the summer months -- as erosion can create a steep drop-off at the end of the trail.

RAIN FOREST TRAIL, LOOPS A & B

This is essentially two trails looping either side of the Pacific Rim Highway. Park in the designated area on the right (west) side of the road. If you are only planning to hike one of the trails, head across the road and hike Loop A. If you have time, hike both short trails to get a better appreciation of the old growth temperate rainforest.

Rain Forest Trail, Loop B

This is the gentler of the two trails. One gradual descent and one ascent present a total of about eighty steps, in different stages. The trail begins at an old clearing where you can see how the trees have managed to re-colonize the logged-off earth. From there the trail leads through a cedar and hemlock thicket and finally into the old growth forest. As you penetrate farther into the forest, all the noises of the highway fade and you are left in total silence. Stop for a moment. Absorb the profound quiet of a classic temperate rainforest.

As you descend you will cross over a bridge made from a single old growth log. Several times along the trail there are excellent viewing sites of a salmon stream that winds its way through the forest. All along the way you will encounter interpretive signs that help explain how the various animals in the rainforest work together with the forest's structure as an ecosystem.

The trail is primarily boardwalk. You can expect to see at least 3 giant cedars including one that is over 800 years old, so don't forget your camera.

Rain Forest Trail, Loop A

Look both ways and be careful crossing the highway (traffic travels surprisingly fast here) and you will find yourself at the beginning of the boardwalk that starts the Loop A trail. This is essentially the same type of old growth forest found on Loop B trail except this route takes you deeper into the gullies of the salmon stream.

TOFINO GUIDE

Expect to encounter about 150 steps on this loop of the trail. The forest is surprisingly open at some points and during the late afternoon the sun will cast long shadows through the massive tree trunks. Catch one of these moments and you will be mesmerized by more shades of the colour green than you ever imagined possible. Watch out for an especially good example of a recently fallen **nurse log** (p. 44), and compare it with another example of a several hundred year old nurse log just a bit farther down the trail.

As on the Loop B trail, you will find interpretive signs as you walk. These signs complement the ones on Loop A, concentrating more on the natural cycles within a temperate rainforest. If you hike both loop trails and absorb all of the information on the signs, you will gain valuable insights into how the ecosystem works in coastal temperate rainforests.

Hiking Time
About 40 minutes per trail.

Length
Loop A Trail: 1 km loop

Loop B Trail: 1 km loop

Location
23.7 km south of Tofino, turn right (west) at the Rain Forest parking sign.

Difficulty
Easy. Loop A Trail has more gullies and stairs than Loop B Trail.

What to do if you see a...

GREY GHOST

Don't be afraid. They're all around you in the forest. Just look up. And they're not dead – not really... not entirely. The silvered, spiky tops of countless trees are the so-called Grey Ghosts of the forest, more poetically called silver snags. This is a natural die-off of the upper sections of western red cedar trees (*Thuja plicata*), regularly occurring on trees that may be green and flourishing in their lower branches. Yes, it probably means that the tree has started to die, but haven't we all? The slow demise of these trees, section by section, could take decades, even centuries, if the tree is left alone. Take notice of the older, persistent Grey Ghosts that have developed three or four spikes curving up in a candelabra shape above the forest canopy. Younger, slender Grey Ghosts are valued by local wood-builders for their elegant lines. If you look closely at the more interesting structures around town you will probably spot some Grey Ghost posts in the local architecture.

National Park Reserve

FLORENCIA BAY BEACH (ALSO CALLED WRECK BAY)

This beach was named after the Peruvian ship *Florencia* that broke up in the bay in November 1860, while being towed back to Victoria from Nootka Sound, having suffered damage in a storm. Prior to 1930, the name Wreck Bay was always used by mariners and locals. The Victoria newspapers wrote much about Wreck Bay in 1900 – 1901 when a brief and frenzied gold rush occurred here, after placer gold was discovered in the black beach sands.

From the Florencia Bay parking lot off the Wick Road (directions below), the trail leading to the beach is only about a 5 minute walk, descending an impressive staircase with about 100 steps.

There are two outstanding features of this beach. The entire length of the long sandy beach is backed by tall clay cliffs that give the beach a remote feeling despite its relatively easy access. Secondly, a number of visually distinct, large boulders dot the edge of the surf. These provide fun exploration opportunities at low tide. An added point of interest can be found approximately two-thirds of the way down the beach to your left (south) where **Gold Mine Trail** emerges from the trees.

Hiking Time
Between 5 and 10 minutes down the steps to the beach.

Length
Short stroll then down about 100 stairs located near the northern end of the beach. The entire beach is about 5 km long.

Location
27.9 km from the Post Office you will arrive at Wick Road on your right. Watch for the Wickaninnish Interpretive Centre sign just before Wick Road. Turn right (west) down Wick Road, then drive 1.4 km to the Florencia Bay sign. Turn left at the sign, drive down

the narrow road a few hundred metres to the last parking lot. If you do not have a Park Pass yet, the nearest place to purchase one is at the Shorepine Bog parking area: about 1.5 km past the Florencia Bay road, turn left.

Difficulty
Easy with many stairs

SHOREPINE BOG TRAIL

This trail is boardwalk all the way, completely flat and wheelchair accessible. It is the easiest walking trail in the park. Because the pine bog ecosystem here presents such a stark contrast to the surrounding rainforest, this trail is definitely one of the most interesting to explore, particularly if you are keen to know more native trees and plants. What makes this area so unusual is the highly acidic condition of the bog, allowing only specific types of vegetation to grow.

Shore pines (*Pinus contorta* var. *contorta*) grow along many rugged coastlines, and frequently take on strange contorted shapes, almost like bonsai trees. In a bog forest, these pines are in a rugged coastal environment, and are deprived of nutrition in the highly acidic and nutrient deficient bog soil. This makes them grow in a stunted fashion, giving them their characteristic rounded shape. Most of the shore pines you see here and along the coast are several hundreds of years old, even though they are not large.

At the start of the trail you will find a Parks Canada booklet in a wooden box providing an excellent natural history of the bog ecosystem. This should help you get to know some of the plants and animals that you can find in the bog forest. One of the more intriguing and elusive plants to look for is the round-leaved sundew; its sticky red droplets catch various types of insects that it ingests. Remember the Venus fly-traps from Grade Six science class? Same design in miniature. If you need help finding a sundew plant, look closely on the ground around the #3 interpretive marker.

Try to make your visit on a dry, sunny day and once you are on the bog pine trail you will feel as if you are on the open tundra. The tall vertical vegetation of the rainforest simply cannot grow in these bogs, although it surrounds them on all sides. This trail makes a good excursion if you want a fairly easy walk and/or a wheelchair accessible trail.

Hiking Time
About 30 minutes

Length
Less than 1 km (loop)

Location
27.9 km from the Post Office to the Wick Road, watching for the Wickaninnish Interpretive Centre sign. Turn right (west) down the road, then 1.5 km past the Florencia Bay sign. Watch for the Shorepine Bog Trail sign.

Difficulty
Very easy. All flat boardwalk. Wheelchair accessible.

National Park Reserve

SOUTH BEACH TRAIL

This trail begins just behind the **Wickaninnish Centre** (p. 79). Watch for the wheelchair ramp and continue south along this path. The beginning is a fairly flat paved trail with ocean viewing benches for the first several hundred metres. All-terrain wheelchairs are available for loan at the Wickaninnish Interpretive Centre; these are well suited for the first 500 metres of this trail. In this time you will pass Lismer Beach, a favourite beach of Arthur Lismer, one of Canada's famous Group of Seven painters. Continuing south, there is a small steep hill and then you continue on a boardwalk. This is where a wheelchair would have to turn back.

After continuing on for about 5 minutes you will pass by another beach on your right that has no official name, so we have nicknamed it **Suds Beach.** The action of the waves and the naturally occurring minerals in the seawater combine to make the beach look like a giant bubble bath. But the real excitement lies ahead, for you are heading towards some of the biggest waves on the West Coast. Just another 5 minutes up the trail you will descend around 30 steps to **South Beach**. You will know that you have arrived at the right place well before you see the beach because of the loud pounding of the surf. This beach is definitely one of the best places to view the **big, BIG waves**. Even on some fairly mild days, because the waves at this beach are funnelled between large rock walls, they create boomers that are at least a metre high.

South Beach is steeply sloped, and made up of very fine pebbles which amplify the classic pounding of the waves and then create a marvellous sound as the waves recede -- **a jingly whooshing noise** -- you really have to hear it to understand. The quality of sea glass on this beach is unsurpassed, but it is hard to find – digging helps. Dark blue is the most sought after sea glass colour, although aquamarine is perhaps lovelier. Another small beach lies further to the south, but cannot compare to this one, so don't bother walking any farther unless you are committed to seeing every possible beach in the area.

Be wary of the headlands on either side and be sure to keep well away from the rocks. As always, resist the temptation to get as close as you can to the ocean, especially near rocky shorelines. **Never turn your back on the Pacific Ocean when you are near its shore**. Read **Rogue Waves**, page 11, for more information.

In past years, the trail has been frequently closed when so-called problem bears forage in the berry-rich area along this trail. The bears are feeding on their natural source of food, and it is unwise to interrupt them. The trail can remain closed until a bear has fed and moved on, which can take hours, sometimes weeks. **Remember, never ever feed or disturb bears**. For more information about black bears, inquire at the **Wickaninnish Centre** and read the important wildlife safety information on page 121.

Hiking Time
About 15 minutes (one way)

Length
1.5 km to the beach, then return

Location
27.9 km from the Post Office to the Wick Road, watching for the Wickaninnish Interpretive Centre sign. Turn right (west) down Wick Road then drive 2.7 km to the parking lot at the end of the road. Stay left and watch for the big Wickaninnish Interpretive Centre signs. Find the trail to the left (west) and behind the Interpretive Centre.

Difficulty
Easy, one small ascent and then descent via stairs

NUU-CHAH-NULTH TRAIL (WICKANINNISH)

This trail links **Florencia Bay** to the southern sections of **Long Beach**. One end of this trail forks off from the **South Beach Trail** beyond the **Wickaninnish Interpretive Centre**. You can follow the directions for South Beach Trail (p. 142) and take the fork on the left (it is marked). From this starting point, the trail will pass through an old growth forest dominated by Sitka spruce.

One small bridge crosses a gully and in rainy months you will have to jump over some fairly large puddles. As the soil becomes more acidic, the forest gives way to a bog that is primarily made up of shore pine. As you walk along the boardwalk, see if you can spot the Labrador tea plant (*Ledum groenlandicum*). Its leaf structure resembles a rhododendron but on a miniature scale. The leaves are fuzzy, with a milky orange colour on the underside.

Originally, Nuu-chah-nulth people used this trail to travel between settlements. After the settlers arrived, they also used the trail, eventually upgrading it by laying wooden posts crossways over the path to provide a firm surface. Bumpy and crude as it was, Model T cars could drive the entire distance of this so-called "corduroy" trail. About half-way along this trail you will see and walk over sections of the original wooden posts crossing the path. After walking over this stretch, an inclining boardwalk will lead you up and out of the bog into a forest that was logged around the turn of the twentieth century. At this point, you can begin to hear the surf of **Florencia Bay**.

After about 10 more minutes of walking you will be at the Florencia Bay parking lot. **This is the other potential starting point of this trail depending on where you choose to park**. Turn right if you want to visit this spectacular beach and take note of a giant cannonball-like rock formation (sandstone concretion) before descending down the stairs toward the beach.

Hiking Time
About 40 minutes

Length
2.5 km one way

Location
27.9 km from the Post Office to the Wick Road, watching for the Wickaninnish Interpretive Centre sign. Turn right (west) down Wick Road then drive 2.7 km to the parking lot at the end of the road. Stay left and watch for the big Wickaninnish Interpretive Centre signs. Find the South Beach trail to the left (west) and behind the Interpretive Centre. The South Beach Trail connects with this trail.

Difficulty
Easy. Mostly boardwalk, a few steps, and some mud

TOFINO GUIDE

GOLD MINE TRAIL

At the time of this update (autumn 2010), the Gold Mine Trail is closed for safety reasons. We include this description in the hope it will eventually re-open.

You might not believe that a trail through a second growth, 40 year old forest could be interesting, yet this is one of the best. In stark contrast to the surrounding old growth forests, this trail leads through an area logged in the 1960s. An attempt to colonize the area with Douglas fir failed because of a lack of specific nutrients in the soil. The forest now growing here is similar to a conifer forest that you would find in eastern North America, very dense with medium sized trees that are struggling to compete for the light. The big difference here is the presence of dozens of enormous stumps, some of them looming overhead, up to 3 metres high. These once were massive 800 year old trees, now they stand like silent sculptures, a reminder of what has been lost.

You will find evidence of logging throughout the Pacific Rim National Park Reserve. Over 20% of this area was logged before it was protected. The most intense logging activity took place during discussions and negotiations leading up to the National Park designation in 1970. This trail bears witness to this logging more vividly than the others in the park.

Near the end of the trail, as you begin to hear the surf of the south end of Florencia Bay, you will walk through a red alder (*Alnus rubra*) forest littered with different species of ferns. This type of growth is typically the earliest plant life to appear in a scarred or altered temperate rainforest ecosystem. The alder wood was used by the aboriginal people to make fishhooks and is still used to smoke salmon.

The trail ends at the mouth of a salmon stream, where you can see iron remnants of old machinery. These date from the turn of the last century when this stream, Lost Shoe Creek, was panned for gold by eager prospectors.

This is not a boardwalk trail so expect mud.

Hiking Time
About 30 minutes (one way)

Length
1 km to the beach, then return

Location
29.1 km south of the Post Office, turn left at the Gold Mine sign

Difficulty
Easy. Flat all the way. May be muddy.

TOFINO GUIDE

What to do if you see a...

VANCOUVER ISLAND MARMOT

First of all, congratulations on finding your way up to 1000 metres elevation (3300 feet) in the Vancouver Island Range, one of the British Columbia's best kept alpine hiking secrets. This white-capped mountain range, visible from Tofino and all along the drive between Port Alberni and Kennedy Lake, is home to one of the world's rarest mammals -- the Vancouver Island Marmot (*Marmota vancouverensis*). The population is so endangered that in 1997 biologists began what they call a genetic lifeboat, capturing a few of the estimated 27 individuals left in the wild to breed in captivity. This program has so far been successful, bringing the wild population back to somewhere between 120 and 140 individuals in 2010. The captive program continues, with more releases expected soon. But alas, they will probably never come down to Tofino!

WILLOWBRAE TRAIL

Around the turn of the last century, this trail served as the overland route between Tofino and various homesteads and settlements to the south. To access the start of the trail drive south, past **The Junction** (where the road to Port Alberni meets the Tofino – Ucluelet road) and turn right (west) on Willowbrae Road. Park in the designated parking lot just after turning off the highway.

You may feel that you are parking in someone's back yard here. Assorted chickens and ducks might be wandering around, but rest assured this is entirely normal. This is not the usual impression of a national park, but the park's Long Beach Unit boundary does extend this far south.

The beginning of the wide, gravel trail is essentially flat, passing through a forest logged at the turn of the last century. There is a Y in the trail as you near the end. Go right to travel to the southern end of **Florencia Bay**. The left-hand route will take you down to **Half Moon Bay**, a small, secluded crescent beach (p. 150).

Hiking Time
About 30 minutes (one way)

Length
1.4 km to Florencia Bay, then return

Location
34.7 km south of the Post Office, turn right on Willowbrae Road and park in the parking area.

Difficulty
Easy: May be muddy.

HALF MOON BAY TRAIL

See the Willowbrae Trail description above. When you reach the small bridge, turn left. This will take you through a dense forest that has formed despite the strong westerly winds that buffet it. About 5 minutes from the bridge, you will find yourself nearing the edge of the forest and it will change to a grove with giant Sitka spruce. These massive trees rely on ocean fog for nearly 20% of their nutrients. After descending a long wooden ramp and steep stairs, you will arrive at a small, crescent-shaped beach. This is the most southerly point in the Long Beach Unit of the Pacific Rim National Park Reserve.

Hiking Time
About 45 minutes one way

Length
Half a kilometre from the small bridge after walking the Willowbrae trail (a total of 2 km from the parking area, one way)

Location
34.7 km south of the Post Office, turn right on Willowbrae Road. Follow Willowbrae Trail to the turnoff described above.

Difficulty
Moderate: About 200 stairs and a wooden ramp

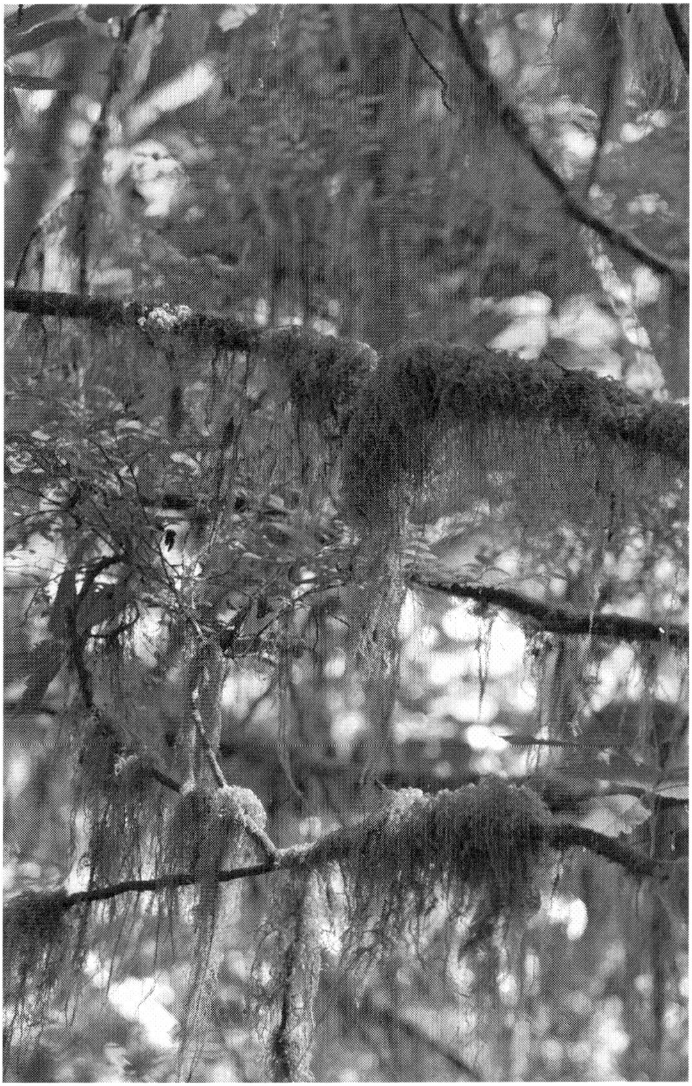

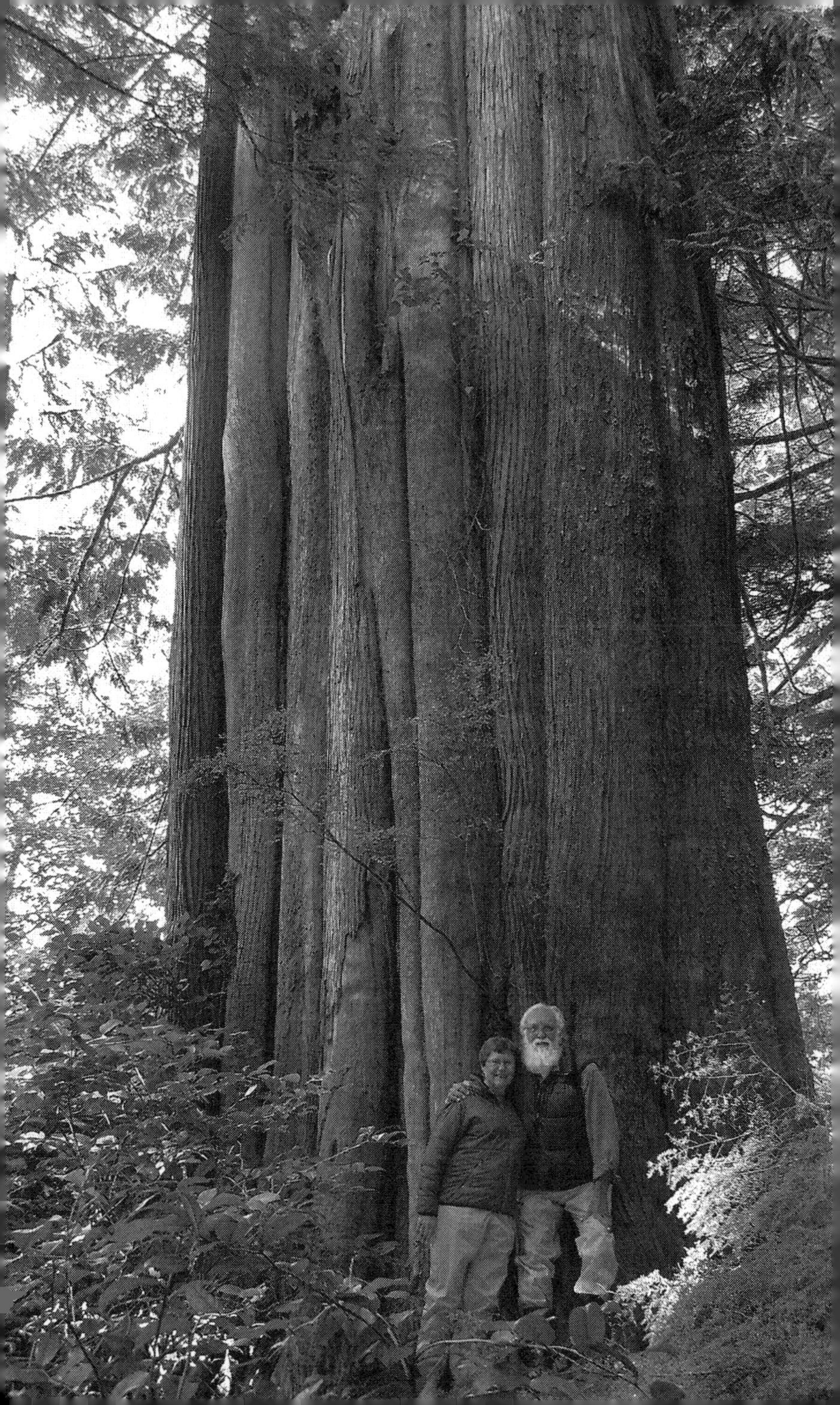

GETTING OFF THE PENINSULA: WILDERNESS EXPLORATION

Experience and Preparation
Self-Guided Sea Kayaking Expeditions
Wildside Heritage Trail (on Flores Island)
Ahous Bay Trail (on Vargas Island)
Big Tree Trail (on Meares Island)
Lone Cone Trail (on Meares Island)

TOFINO GUIDE

EXPERIENCE AND PREPARATION

The waterways in Clayoquot Sound are notoriously difficult to navigate. If you are planning a boating trip around the Tofino area, **you should be an experienced wilderness traveller** and have a good knowledge of ocean currents, coastal weather and marine safety. At the very least, please remember a few important safety notes:

- Be keenly aware of the tides, which can rise and fall at surprising rates. Remember to bring a tide chart.
- The currents created by the tidal fluctuations can be fierce. **Many an unsuspecting kayaker magically moves backwards in Clayoquot Sound's waters**, despite a strong forward paddle stroke. If you have not experienced ocean currents, best to get a few pointers from folks at the local kayak shop or better, go with a guide.
- Hidden reefs are plentiful and dangerous and the wind can pick up unexpectedly.
- The difference between the protected inlet waters and the unprotected open ocean is enormous. **Local boaters are often chastened by the open waters**, even on seemingly calm days.

If you are planning on landing at any remote area, be prepared:

- Black bears, wolves and cougars live in Clayoquot Sound. Thankfully, there have been very few incidents where animals have become pests in our region. We prefer to keep it that way, so please make sure to **take great care with your food and garbage**. Quite simply: if you pack it in, pack it out. If you are camping never ever leave food exposed and unattended.

- If you are planning to land on Vargas or Flores Island, talk to someone with a current understanding of the wildlife situation, as there have been a few close encounters with wolves in the recent past. Start by phoning BC Parks: www.bcparks.ca.
- **Always let someone know where you are going and when you expect to be back**. Remember to check with your contact on your return.
- **Always inform yourself about land tenure wherever you go. Do not presume you can camp wherever you want**. What may seem to be uninhabited wilderness in your eyes could be private or tribal land. Camping on Indian Reserves is prohibited (marked IR on marine charts). Permission from First Nations band office may be required for camping in traditional territory outside IRs (p. 38 for First Nation contact numbers). There is very little private land in Clayoquot Sound, but it is important to be aware of this designation also. Watch for and be respectful of private land signs, and if you see a cabin, please respect the occupant's privacy and stay away.
- A large portion of Clayoquot Sound's coastline is designated as Provincial Park. Camping is permitted within most of the Provincial Park boundaries, but you should check their website for closures before planning an expedition: www.bcparks.ca.
- You are reading *Tofino Guide*, so you know the importance of consulting a good guide. There are several guide books detailing wilderness exploration in Clayoquot Sound. See **Recommended Reading** (p. 255) to find the guidebook best suited to your adventure.

TOFINO GUIDE

SELF-GUIDED SEA KAYAKING EXPEDITIONS

> If you are an experienced kayaker looking for adventure, you've come to the right place. Tofino has a kayak launch at the bottom of First Street to the left (west) of the dock (p. 116). Long term parking is available at Main Street and Third. There is usually a fee for long term parking – watch for signs or inquire at the District of Tofino office: 121 Third Street, 250-725-3229. For information about kayak tours, see p. 96.

WILDSIDE HERITAGE TRAIL (ON FLORES ISLAND)

For centuries, the Ahousaht people used sections of this trail to reach the wild beaches on the west side of Flores Island. In 1995, under the guidance of the Ahousaht elders, a 16 km trail was completed to expand the economic opportunities in Ahousaht traditional territory. In 2009 BC Parks and other project partners began working with the Ahousaht First Nation to continue the trail repairs and to develop a more robust ecotourism strategy for Ahousaht and Flores Island.

The results of these ambitious projects are superb. The Wildside Heritage Trail now winds its way through ancient Sitka spruce forests and visits two of the most spectacular beaches in Clayoquot Sound: **Whitesands Beach** and **Cow Bay**. This is a long trail, so bring a backpack with provisions and be prepared for some mud and spontaneous weather changes. Most hikers choose to camp for a night or two on Cow Bay, the final beach on the trail.

Most of the trail alternates between open sandy beach and boardwalks over the headlands, but a few sections in the forest have no boardwalk and may be muddy. Excellent interpretive signs along the entire trail point out culturally modified trees

(p. 43), historical landmarks and valuable insights to the indigenous culture.

If you are camping at Cow Bay, you might be interested in exploring the trail up **Mount Flores** (902 m), the highest point on Flores Island. The beginning of the trail is located at the northern end of Cow Bay, the last beach on the Wildside Heritage Trail. The first kilometre of the Mount Flores trail is well marked, but fallen trees and thick brush begin to obscure the trail after this. Because of its obscurity, **only attempt the Mount Flores hike if you are an experienced navigator**, preferably with a GPS. Do not attempt this hike late in the day.

Length
16 km one way, then return

Location and Transportation
To access this trail, you need to take a 40 minute boat ride or a 10 minute seaplane flight (p. 95) from Tofino to **Marktosis**, the Ahousaht village on Flores Island. The scheduled water taxi, *Ahousaht Pride*, departs Tofino at 10:30 am and 4:00 pm from **First Street Dock** and costs $20 one way (cash only). Return departures leave Marktosis at 8:30 am and 1:00 pm.

There is a $20 fee per person (cash only) for accessing the trail, payable at the Ahousaht Band Office in Marktosis. These fees pay for trail staff and maintenance needed along the extensive boardwalk system. Some water taxi or charter operators may offer to drop you off on the middle of the trail to avoid the trail fee but we strongly discourage this.

The Band Office is located just south of the arrival dock in a two-story red wooden building. The staff at the Band Office will point you to the trailhead, down the road (south) that led you to the Band Office, staying left at the fork. Nuu-chah-nulth guides are occasionally available to guide hikers. Call the **Ahousaht Band Office** 250-670-9531 for guide arrangements and any other questions about the Wildside Heritage Trail and Marktosis tourism information.

TOFINO GUIDE

For accommodation in Marktosis phone **Vera's Little Guest House** at 250-670-9511.

For alternate water taxi arrangements phone Cougar Island Water Taxi at 888-726-8427

Hiking Time
5 hours one way. Recommended as an overnight wilderness camping trip. Hiking the trail in one day is possible, but requires an early morning seaplane ride to Marktosis and a chartered boat or seaplane ride home.

Difficulty
Moderate. There is very little elevation gain, but the wilderness setting demands some hiking experience and agility. **The final trail up Mount Flores is difficult and recommended only for fit, experienced hikers with a GPS.**

AHOUS BAY TRAIL (ON VARGAS ISLAND)

To access the Ahous Bay Trail from the calm, inside waters of Clayoquot Sound, you must be a guest at the Vargas Island Inn, because the trailhead starts on the Inn's private property. If you prefer to go with a guided group, **Tofino Sea Kayaking Company** offers two-night kayaking tours with lodging at the Vargas Island Inn: phone 250-725-4222 or www.tofino-kayaking.com for more information.

The Vargas Island Inn is owned and operated by a family whose ancestors homesteaded on this waterfront property in the early 1900s. Access to a wood-fired sauna and to the outdoor shower house is included with your stay at this waterfront wilderness resort. The trail to Ahous Bay starts immediately off the back deck of the inn and is completely flat for the entire 2.5 km.

The trail is mostly open, but it is not regularly maintained so you should continually watch for ribbons marking the route as you hike. There are some small stream crossings near the end of the trail where you may have to get your boots wet if you cannot navigate around them.

In about 45 minutes you will arrive at Ahous Bay, a long sandy beach several kilometres in length, facing the open Pacific. The trail emerges onto the southern part of the beach and if you walk north (right), near the end of the beach you will cross over a fresh water estuary with fast, clear, running water. This is a wonderful location for frolicking and observing many species of animals and birds. .

This beach is spectacular. Few people visit it, so you will probably experience splendid isolation and find many beach treasures. You may see hundreds of sand dollars at a time on this beach, and at the north end, you can usually find the smooth olive shells that make crafty necklaces.

TOFINO GUIDE

Ahous Bay is a favourite feeding ground for grey whales so be sure to find a good spot on the beach and watch for their spouts (binoculars help). If you see a few boats floating near each other in the bay, these are probably whale watching boats, and a definite sign that whales are out there.

Remember to give yourself enough time to get back to the inn before sunset.

For accommodation information and reservations phone Vargas Island Inn: 250-725-3309.

If you wish to access Ahous Bay but are not a guest at the inn, you must navigate the 5 km of dangerous waters between Tofino and Ahous Bay. See Canadian Hydrographic Service Nautical Chart #3673 for location and route finding.

Hiking Time
About 1 hour (one way)

Length
2.5 km one way

Location
Vargas Island, about a 1-3 hour paddle by kayak or a 15 minute boat ride that may be arranged with your accommodation.

Difficulty
Easy. Very flat with some narrow bridges. Lots of mud most of the year. Route finding may be a bit challenging at times so keep your eyes open and watch for trail markers.

What to do if you see a...

WOLF

Stand still and marvel. This rarely happens. Leave it or them alone, do not disturb or follow. If the animal is too close for comfort, make eye contact and back away slowly.

The Vancouver Island wolf (*Canis lupus crassodon*) is an endangered subspecies of the gray wolf. It is common for individuals to be different colours, from black, through various grey tones and even white. Roaming in packs of 5 to 20, they mainly live off the island's resident Columbian black-tailed deer.

Wolves are a vital part of Clayoquot Sound's ecosystem and it is a treat to be in a place where there is a healthy population of these large predators. Sadly, this may be changing. There have been occasional reports of wolves approaching campers on the beaches of Vargas Island. This is disheartening for two reasons: 1) the situation is completely avoidable by keeping your campsite clear of food scraps; 2) this behaviour means that the wolves may need to be killed for the safety of future campers.

Wolves conditioned to humans are the only wolves that are dangerous. If a wolf approaches you and does not show signs of fear (again, this would be astonishingly rare), make yourself as big as possible, and be aggressive by making noise and showing the animal that you are dangerous. Avoid the urge to run away.

See page 121 for more information about wolf encounters.

TOFINO GUIDE

BIG TREE TRAIL (ON MEARES ISLAND)

When you travel by boat from Tofino to the start of this trail, you will pass over or around (depending on the tide) the extensive mud flats of **Lemmens Inlet**. These are critical resting and feeding grounds for migrating shorebirds on the West Coast.

Just before you land on Meares, the last small island you pass is **Morpheus Island**. This island has been used for centuries as a traditional tribal burial ground. From the turn of the last century until the 1950s Morpheus Island also became the official Tofino Cemetery. It is now under the guardianship of Tofino, with the condition that no one else be buried there.

The start of the Big Tree Trail is a boardwalk, well-maintained by First Nations and guiding companies. After 15 minutes, the boardwalk ends and you find yourself on a trail. From here, trail conditions vary with the weather and season. This latter section is a muddy walk if it has been raining, or if you are hiking between October and May.

As you ascend a small hill, you will notice a wide body of water to your left – this is Lemmens Inlet. This inlet runs up the middle of Meares, which is a horseshoe shaped island. Boaters often mistake this inlet as a route through to Vancouver Island. Seafood lovers may be interested to know that Lemmens Inlet is a major commercial oyster growing area. Tours of the oyster farms are available one day per year during the **Clayoquot Oyster Festival** (www.oystergala.com) on the third weekend of November.

About 300 metres after you start walking on the boardwalk you will be in the company of ancients. Several big western red cedars on this trail will loom in front of you, like the Hanging Garden Tree, some 600 metres from the trail's beginning. This emblem of Clayoquot held the title of the largest western red cedar in Canada during the mid 1980s. Sadly, more precise measuring techniques have stripped it of this distinction. **The age of the giants on this trail ranges from 1000 to 1500 years old**. These are some of the oldest and largest life forms on earth. *Read that last sentence again.*

All visitors to the Big Tree Trail are required to purchase a Tribal Park Pass. The pass is $3 per person for those arriving by kayak or canoe or $5 per person for those arriving in a fuel-powered vessel. The revenues generated go directly to the Tla-o-qui-aht Tribal Parks initiative (www.tribalparks.ca). Most tour companies automatically add this to the tour price, but ask your tour operator if you are not sure. If you are arriving at the trail unguided, each person in your party should bring $3 (cash only). The money is collected by a Tribal Parks worker at or along the trail. A Tribal Park worker may not be available to collect your fee, depending on the season and staff availability. It is accepted practice to use the trail if there is no Tribal Parks staff on-site.

Location
Midway along Morpheus Island's west side, find the trailhead in a small cove on Meares Island, directly opposite Morpheus. Look for kayaks.

You can access this trail in several ways. You can go on a guided kayak tour (p. 96) or a cultural tour (p. 94), you can hire a water taxi (p. 242) or you can paddle yourself. See the other sections of this guide for specifics of these various options. Anchorage is difficult and crowded at the small landing near the trailhead. Only attempt to bring your own motor vessel here if you are an experienced mariner confident of getting ashore in challenging tidal conditions. Vessels over 7 metres in length are not suitable to the anchorage here.

Hiking and Travel Time
Water taxi travel to Meares Island takes about 10 minutes (one way). Kayaking travel to Meares Island takes about 45 minutes, depending on your skill level.

The boardwalk section of the hike takes about 20 minutes, one way. The entire loop trail takes about 1.5 hours. Budget at least an extra hour in your itinerary for giant tree gazing and photo opportunities.

Length
The boardwalk portion is less than 1 km. The full loop is 3 km. The loop option is often closed for trail upgrades, especially during winter months. If this is the case, respect the rope boundary and turn around at the end of the boardwalk.

Difficulty
Moderate: Expect mud and some route finding. **The boardwalk-only portion is easy.**

LONE CONE TRAIL (ON MEARES ISLAND)

Contrary to local lore, Lone Cone is *not* an old volcano, though it certainly does look like one. A prominent landmark in Clayoquot Sound, its looming presence dominates Tofino Harbour. A trail leads up the south side of the cone. **This trail is extremely steep and unrelenting**, making this one of the most challenging and rewarding trails in Clayoquot Sound.

The trailhead is accessed through private property and is difficult to find. In order to hike this trail, **we recommend you hire a guide** (**Ocean Outfitters**, 250-725-2866, www.oceanoutfitters.bc.ca) or call the **Tla-o-qui-aht Band Office** 250-725-3233 for details about permission and how to locate the trailhead.

From its summit, Lone Cone provides an impressive 360 degree panorama. All of Clayoquot Sound lies at your feet, no other view of the area can compare.

Hiking Time
About 2.5 hours straight up, 3 hours down

Length
About 1 mostly-vertical km each direction

Difficulty
Difficult. Endurance and pain tolerance required.

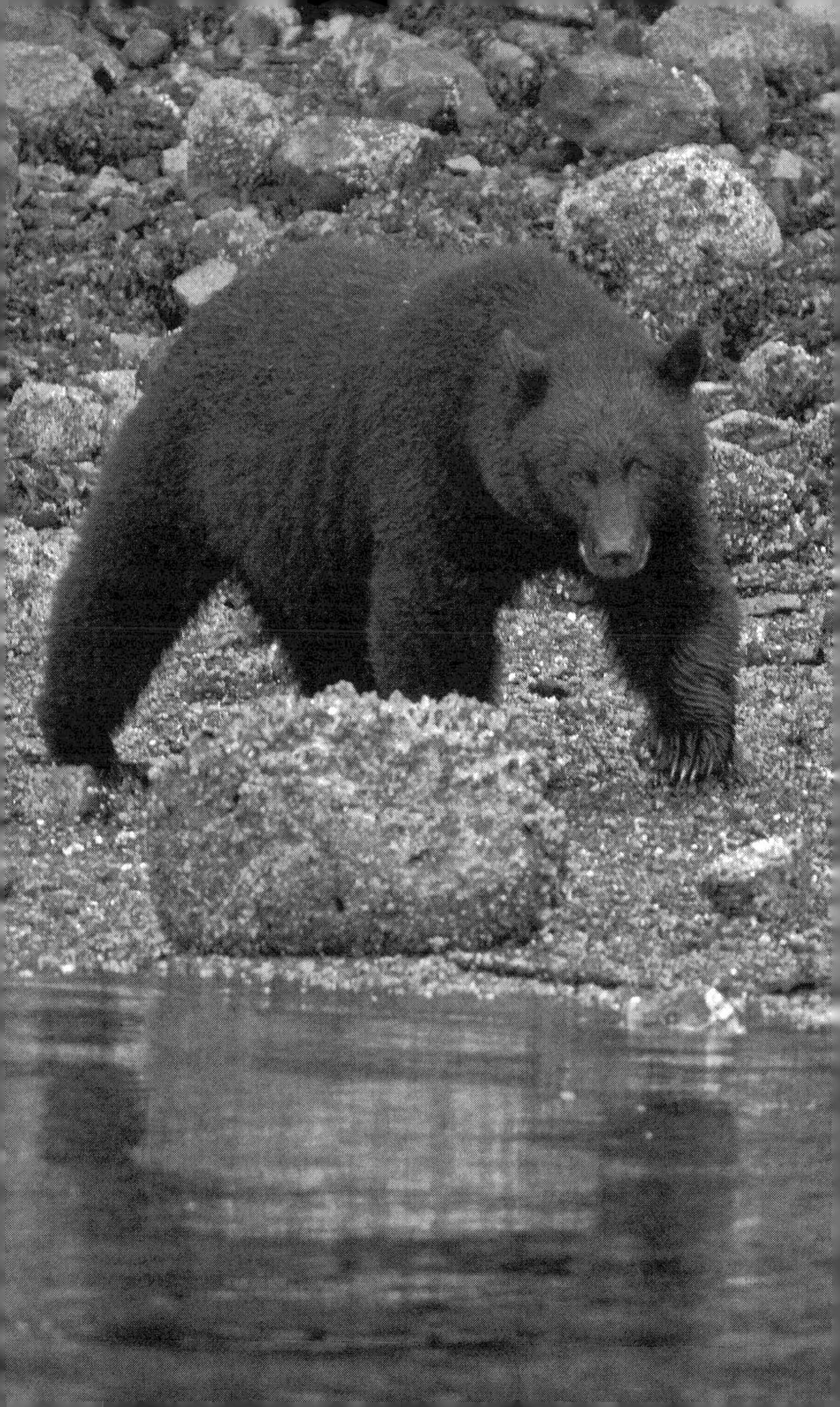

FOOD, DRINK AND DINING OUT

Take-out and Casual Eateries

Pubs and Lounges

Finer Dining

Beer, Wine and Liquor Sales

Catering

Seafood Stores

Foraging for Tofino's Seafood

Purchasing a Fishing License (Yes, you need this for shellfish, too!)

Check for Red Tide before Harvesting Shellfish

Can I eat the Mussels?

Where can I find Clams in Clayoquot Sound?

Finding Oysters in Clayoquot Sound

What about live Crabs?

TOFINO GUIDE

TAKE-OUT AND CASUAL EATERIES

The Back Nine Bar and Grill
1850 Pacific Rim Highway, 250-725-3332,
www.longbeachgolfcourse.com

The Back Nine Bar and Grill is worth the trip out to **Long Beach Golf Course** (p. 214), even if you have no idea why golfers chase around those little white balls. The menu is mostly standard pub fare, with good salads and an excellent chicken burger. If you have children, you will appreciate the 18-hole mini golf course adjacent to the restaurant while you relax with a beer or tea and watch your play kids play from a safe distance.

Meal prices start in the $12 range.

Big Daddy's Fish Fry
411 Campbell Street, 250-725-4415

Big Daddy's serves yummy fish and chips and has a splendid burger selection too. Choose from tempura battered salmon, cod or halibut with home-cut French fries. The popcorn shrimp is a tasty deep-fried side. There is also a selection of soups and salads. The picnic tables in front of the shack can be overcrowded, but the Village Green across the street is open to the public and has a covered gazebo with plenty of space to sit and eat.

Meal prices start around $12

Breakers Deli
430 Campbell Street in The Campbell House building,
250-725-2558, www.breakersdeli.com

Breakers prepares their homemade foods fresh in-house each day. When possible, they use free run meats, fresh local herbs, organic veggies and free range eggs. This is a great stop for a soup and sandwich or a wrap. The breakfast menu is also scrumptious, featuring homemade granola and original breakfast wraps. You can also purchase specialty cheeses, dips and salsas along with fresh baked breads. Do not miss the cookies under the take-out counter.

Take-out and counter seating, meals start around $10.

Caffe Vincente
441 Campbell Street, 250-725-2599

With urban design, tiled floors, and a steaming espresso machine this café has a distinctive bistro feeling. The Americano is rich and dark, with a smooth natural creaminess on top. Vincente's is locally famous for its Big Gun sandwich, served on a croissant or bagel, costing about $9. Expect other café-like food items, like soups and salads in the $8 - $12 range. A good stop, particularly on a rainy day as there is ample room to relax at the tables or in in their comfy chair zone.

Free wireless internet with purchase, 2 computer terminals for hire.

Chocolate Tofino
1180 Pacific Rim Highway, 725-2526, www.chocolatetofino.com

To call these delectable nuggets chocolate is not fair; handmade food jewels is a more apt description. Take a box home and devour a few in the parking lot on your way out. The Chocolate Shop, as it's locally known, also serves to-die-for ice cream and gelato in home-made waffle cones. If you are lucky and/or very charming they will drip fresh chocolate on top of your ice cream cone – just ask to test out this theory. Anticipate $5 for a splendid hit of chocolate or a home-made ice cream cone.

Common Loaf Bake Shop
180 First Street, 725-3915

A hip meeting place for everyone who is coming and going (and just plain staying) in town. The bulletin board is a cultural icon, often more informative than the village newspaper. Tofino's most famous bakery is still pounding the dough after almost twenty years and continues to attract the most eclectic mix of folks you will find anywhere in Clayoquot Sound. Freshly baked Peasant Bread and Common Loaf's Sourdough are popular loaves of choice. At lunch and dinner, they serve entrees, salads, soup and pizza by the slice, with wine and beer available. Head upstairs to enjoy the view.

Counter service, meals start around $8

Driftwood Lounge at the Wickaninnish Inn
Osprey Lane or enter by foot off North Chesterman Beach, 250-725-3106, www.wickinn.com

The Driftwood Lounge may be Tofino's best kept secret. If you're walking along North Chesterman Beach (p. 66) towards the Wickaninnish Inn, make a point to wander into this delightful little café right off the beach. Breakfast and lunch are both excellent. The coffee is exceptional and the sandwiches are served on their house-made bread (baked daily) and are some of the best in town. Despite the great food and drink served in a casual setting, you will find it all takes a backseat to the stunning beach-side setting and the fabulous décor.

Table service, meals start around $12

Fiesta Taco
421 Main Street, 250-725-2177

"Tofino's own Tex-Mex experience" has the menu that you'd expect from such a claim: bean, chicken, veggie and fish burritos and tacos; enchiladas; fajitas and tostadas. On the "Tex" side of the things, a good half-pound burger costs $7. Surprisingly, this is a great place for a good breakfast in a calm setting: bacon, eggs and a few home fries are only $6.

Eat-in or take-out counter service, the prices are tough to beat, starting at $6 for a good meal.

Gary's Kitchen
308 Neill Street, 250-725-3921

This is Tofino's version of traditional Chinese eat-in or take-out. Chicken Balls and Egg Rolls are standard Chinese fare, plus you'll find diner-style items like burgers and fish and chips on the menu for anyone in your party wishing to stay in the comfort zone of North American food. If you want it fast, fried and inexpensive this is the place to go. Gary's is usually populated with locals during the week around lunch break, which makes it a good place for visiting social scientists to witness a cross section of our town.

Table service, meals start around $8

The Hot Dog Guy
Campbell Street at Fourth, the white tent in-between Sugar Shack and Storm Surf Shop

No fast food joints exist in Tofino, but this hot dog guy comes close. Good quality sausages as well as generic hot dogs with all the fixings are served fast and with jovial hot dog stand flair. The cart is located under a small white event tent at Campbell Street and Fourth on the Sugar Shack's lawn. The convenient location of a hot dog stand next to an ice cream shop makes it a popular stop for families looking for a quick kid-pleasing bite. If you're a sausage lover, try the Vancouver Island sausage or the chorizo.

Order at the cart, sausages start at about $4

Jupiter Juicery & Bakeshop
451 Main Street, 250-725-4226

Located in the bottom floor of the big yellow building between Campbell and Main at Fourth Street, Jupiter Juice is the undisputed king of fruit smoothies and fresh veggie juices. If you're really lucky, you might happen upon Al's legendary raspberry and white chocolate chunk muffins. French style baguettes and good sandwiches. Mini pizzas baked daily.

Take-out counter service, sandwiches start around $7

TOFINO GUIDE

The Sugar Shack
450 Campbell Street at Fourth

A wide selection of ice cream and gelato flavours and the option to add sprinkles makes this a favourite stop for kids. They also serve good espresso-based coffee, milk shakes, and usually have an assortment of other treats on display to satisfy your sweetest cravings. Expect to pay about $4 for a good ice cream cone.

Tacofino
1180 Pacific Rim Highway, 250-725-8228, www.tacofino.com

This orange take-out bus is located at the back of the **Live to Surf** parking lot. The menu is straightforward: burritos and tacos with pork, beef, chicken, bean or fish. The food is good, and the freshly squeezed vegetable/fruit juices stand alone as exceptional menu items. The veggie burrito is a thrifty favourite at $6.

Outdoor seating or take-out from the counter service, prices start at about $6

Tofino Tea Bar
346 Campbell Street at Second, 250-725-8833,
www.tofinoteabar.com

Tea lovers rejoice: Tofino has its own dedicated tea lounge. With a staggering array of premium loose-leaf teas, this place pleases the most discerning tea drinkers. They also have assorted pastries to nibble with your tea, and tea making accessories for sale.

Tofitian Internet Café
1180 Pacific Rim Highway, www.tofitian.com

Located in the **Live to Surf** parking lot. If you are close to the beaches area and looking for a quick and good cup of coffee, this is the place to go. The pleasant glass-covered patio is usually has local surfers milling about discussing swell heights and wetsuit thicknesses. There are usually a few tasty pastries for sale, but no food service.

Free wireless internet with purchase, 3 computer terminals for hire

Tony's Pizza & Donairs
131 First Street, 250-725-2121

This is the only pizza joint in town and thankfully it is good pizza! Ask if they have the second pizza at half price special, and make sure you get a cookie – they're fantastic. Limited stool seating is available, but if you'd rather stay home and order in, they have a fast delivery service. Tony's also serves and delivers other to-go foods like donairs. The place gets busy around meal times, so it's best to call ahead and order.

Slices around $5, Pizzas around $20

Tuff Beans
461 Campbell Street, 250-725-4246, www.tuffbeans.com

This casual eatery is open early for breakfast. Both breakfast and lunch are ordered from the counter and then delivered to your table or booth. This is a favourite spot for local boat dwellers and marine workers, because of its close proximity to Fourth Street Dock and its reasonable prices. Tuff Beans is one of your best bets for a casual breakfast and a good drip or espresso-based coffee derived from our favourite Kicking Horse Coffee. The breakfast bagel is a local favourite for a quick, inexpensive breakfast. On a sunny day, take your food out to the patio and gawk at local traffic in the four-way stop intersecting Fourth and Campbell Street. Or look over the street to the views of **Meares Island** and beyond.

Free wireless internet with purchase, 3 computer terminals for hire

Lunch items around $10, Breakfast items around $8

TOFINO GUIDE

Wildside Grill
1180 Pacific Rim Highway, 250-725-9453, www.wildsidegrill.com

At first glance you might dismiss this modest shack in the **Live to Surf** parking lot, but take our advice and pay attention. The two owners -- a commercial fisherman and a professional chef -- have taken seafood to a new level. The salmon, halibut or cod are panko crusted creating a delightfully crispy fish, not at all greasy. The fish and chips are terrific, and the other menu items are mouth watering. If you get a chance, try the fish tacos, the bison burger and the won ton soup. Good breakfast sandwiches are also served, but unfortunately you have to wait until 10:00 am to get them.

Meals start around $11

PUBS AND LOUNGES

Dockside Pub
634 Campbell (at Weigh West Marine Resort), 250-725-3277, www.weighwest.com

With a casual atmosphere and a great view, this pub is located below the Weigh West Marine Resort and next to the Blue Heron Restaurant. There are about 65 seats, a jukebox in the corner, pool table, and multiple television screens. The daily specials include appetizers, soups, sandwiches, and pastas. This is a favourite local hangout, especially during sporting events, and is good place for a burger, nacho or wings. This is Tofino's version of a sports bar.

Meals start around $12

Sandbar Pub
If you are looking to whoop it up after 10 pm, this is the place to go to dance and drink. Locally referred to as the Maquinna, the Sandbar Pub is located in the downstairs of the Maquinna Hotel at First and Main Street. There is a pool table and plenty of smiling faces.

Shelter
601 Campbell Street, 250-725-3733, www.shelterrestaurant.com

Shelter does an exceptional job providing both pub food and fine dining. For information about fine dining at Shelter, see page 179. If you are looking for a pub-like atmosphere, walk in the door, turn right and sit at the comfortable booth seats or at the bar and surrounding small tables. The Lounge Menu delivers an assortment of good burgers, pizza, and the popular Teriyaki Street Bowl with salmon and chicken, veggies and rice. If you like calamari, order their generous portion to share with at least one other person. Multiple televisions show a variety of surf and skateboard videos, unless there is a Vancouver Canucks hockey game, in which case the place is packed for viewing.

Meals start around $14

FINER DINING

Blue Heron Restaurant
634 Campbell Street, 250-725-4266, www.weighwest.com

Just outside the central core of Tofino, you will find the Weigh West Marine Resort on the Meares Island side of the highway. Go past the main hotel office and down the steep hill to find the restaurant on your right, at the water's edge. Watch for river otters often playing just off the docks here, and the blue heron patiently waiting for fish.

The menu is straightforward and the food is tasty and fresh. Appetizers like shrimp, calamari or chicken wings are offered in the $10 range. The main courses are in the mid-$20 range. You will find a variety of burgers to choose from, and good fries (including yam fries). The location is outstanding, perched over the inlet waters, raised on piers. You can imagine the fish swimming below you as you dine. Lovely.

Chuckling Oyster
1254 Pacific Rim Highway, 250-725-2323, www.c-orca.com

Located near Chesterman Beach in the Clayoquot Orca Lodge, this restaurant and lounge provides a welcome evening getaway if you want to escape the busy downtown restaurant scene. There are two seating areas, the lounge and the dining room. The décor is somewhat dated, but the ambiance of the place is comfortable. One menu services the two seating areas with a variety of standard surf and turf items. There is a full bar and a fireplace to warm your soggy feet on rainy nights.

Lounge-style entrees around $15, finer dining entrees around $26

Long Beach Lodge (on Cox Bay)
1441 Pacific Rim Highway, 250-725-2442,
www.longbeachlodgeresort.com

This resort opened in April 2002 and its restaurant instantly became a local favourite. With its beach front location and sweeping ocean view to the lighthouse on Lennard Island, the setting is relaxed, despite the lodge's grand interior. The restaurant is split in two sections: you choose to sit in the spacious and casual Great Room or in the more formal dining room. The menu is extensive here, ranging from a variety of wood-fired pizzas (about $16) to Peace River Country Bison Osso Buco (about $31). The comfortable couches and lounge chairs in the Great Room are popular with guests at the lodge, and with visitors and local residents, all of whom appreciate the view, the extensive wine cellar and the good beer on tap. Be sure to phone several days ahead to secure dinner reservations.

Lounge-style entrees around $15, finer dining entrees around $28

Pointe Restaurant, at the Wickaninnish Inn
Osprey Lane, 250-725-3106, www.wickinn.com

Located 5 km south of Tofino off the Pacific Rim Highway, the Wickaninnish Inn and its featured restaurant have been busy building a world class reputation since opening in 1996. The restaurant is situated almost precariously on a bluff overlooking Chesterman Beach. A large copper-hooded fireplace dominates the centre of the dining room, and tables are positioned along a wall of floor-to-ceiling windows. The stunning views entice patrons to bring their cameras to the dining room, so they can discreetly snap photos of the summer sunsets as they dine.

All of the dinner entrees are around $30 and the appetizers are between $15 and $20. The seasonal menus are usually weighted toward seafood, but you will always find at least one poultry and one red meat dish. If you are lucky enough to catch it on the menu, try the **Pan Seared Lingcod & Braised Pacific Octopus.** Be sure to phone several days ahead to secure dinner reservations.

Entrées around $30

TOFINO GUIDE

The Schooner on Second
331 Campbell Street, 250-725-3444, www.schoonerrestaurant.ca

Look for the big maroon building with the ship jutting out of the back. The interior of this veteran Tofino restaurant carries the theme further, with the decor giving you the feeling of dining inside a sailing vessel. The dinner menu relies mostly on fresh seafood, but there are enough non-seafood choices for those looking for alternatives. This is a popular breakfast spot for Tofino residents and visitors, and it is also open for lunch in a casual, pub-like atmosphere. Their signature dinner dish, Halibut Bawden Bay, is a great choice: a plump halibut filet split and stuffed with crab, shrimp, brie cheese and pine nuts.

Dinner entrees priced from $20-$36. Breakfast and lunch items start around $12.

Sea Shanty
300 Main Street, 250-725-2902, www.himwitsa.com

Located inside the **House of Himwitsa** building, almost every table here commands a spectacular view of Tofino harbour. From here you look over the harbour to many local landmarks: Opitsaht Village, Meares Island, Stubbs Island, and even a slice of Vargas Island is visible. The restaurant and adjoining art gallery and lodge are First Nations owned and operated. Sea Shanty is open for three meals and is a great spot to look out over the harbour for a relaxed breakfast. The lunch menu is standard pub fare, with good battered halibut and chips. The dinner menu focuses on local seafood, featuring specials like The Echachis: shellfish complemented with ginger and sambuca cream sauce set on a bed of linguini. But non-fish-eaters need not dismay – the classic 8oz or 10oz ribeye steak is fire grilled and super tasty.

Dinner Entrée prices around $20, Breakfast and lunch start around $12

Shelter
601 Campbell Street, 250-725-3733, www.shelterrestaurant.com

If you're looking for the old Crab Bar, you've found it. In 2003, Shelter Restaurant took over the premises of this old Tofino favourite and transformed it into one of Tofino's most popular restaurants. For information about the comfortable seating in the lounge, see Shelter description under Pubs, page 175. The fireside seats and the upstairs section have intimate candlelit dining. On summer nights, the outdoor heated patio offers a prospect overlooking the famous **Eik Tree** (p. 45) and Clayoquot Sound.

Shelter serves lunch and dinner from an eclectic menu. A popular lunch item is the Halibut Burger, which arrives garnished with a giant deep-fried onion ring. The calamari is a local favourite, best shared with two or more friends. The dinner menu spans the surf and turf spectrum but one of the more popular items is the Marinated Double-Cut Pork Chop.

Entrée prices around $25. Lounge menu prices around $15

SOBO
311 Neill Street at First, 250-725-2341, www.sobo.ca

In its early days, the famous purple SOBO bus served amazing food-to-go to an ever-growing lineup of hungry Tofino visitors and locals who became addicted to feature items like polenta fries and bean burritos. Today this celebrated eatery has outgrown its wheels, left behind the take-out bus and now serves a full lunch and dinner menu. Their new location is downtown, just across from the **Common Loaf Bake Shop**.

SOBO (short for Sophisticated Bohemian which sums up their culinary style) is famous for its Killer Fish Taco and Crispy Shrimp Cakes, both exceptional if you are in for lunch. Expect excellent fresh salads and soups. The Duck Two Ways is a favourite dinner entrée. Parents will appreciate the play area on the back patio, a structure honouring the old SOBO bus imaginatively constructed by a local father. This outdoor nook is a happy place for the little ones while the parents sip pints of great beer on tap or excellent espresso drinks. Have lunch with kids in relative peace.

Lunch menu prices about $14, Dinner menu entrees about $24

Spotted Bear Bistro
120 Fourth Street at Campbell, 250-725-2215,
www.spottedbearbistro.com

The much celebrated **Raincoast Café** closed in 2008 and the Spotted Bear Bistro has done an exceptional job of taking over this space. Since this restaurant opened, its simple, elegant dinner menu has impressed residents, visitors and reviewers. The restaurant is quite small, so you will be close to neighbouring tables if it is busy. If your menu choice is from the sea, expect a fresh and original treat, like the smoked tuna bacon that accompanies the salmon main. The beef striploin with a whole grain mustard sauce is superb. The bistro only serves dinner. A reservation is recommended June through September and year round on weekends.

Entrees start around $26

Calm Waters Restaurant at the Tin Wis Resort
1119 Pacific Rim Highway, 250-725-4445, www.tinwis.com

The Tin Wis hotel and restaurant are owned and operated by the Tla-o-qui-aht First Nation, whose traditional territory includes Tofino and the immediate surrounding area. The owners' influence is pleasantly reflected in the building design, interior motifs and background music. In the Tla-o-qui-aht language, Tin Wis translates as calm waters. Accordingly, the ocean tends to be unusually calm in front of this restaurant, creating a relaxed ambience. With music playing softly as you dine, you can sense another time and another reality. The Tin Wis serves an excellent breakfast. If you're a hungry teenager or eat like one, try to eat your way through Tla-o-qui-aht Warrior, an impressively large and tasty breakfast. The dinner menu is a cultural adventure, bringing "the traditional ways of the Nuu-chah-nulth People to share with you the experience of exquisite blends of Ancient spirit and contemporary West Coast cuisine." The restaurant is closed for lunch.

Dinner entrees around $24. Breakfast items start around $12.

Tough City Sushi & Crab Bar
350 Main Street, 250-725-2021, www.toughcity.com

Offering a full sushi menu and Japanese-style entrees on the waterfront, Tough City Sushi has grown every year in sophistication and size. July and August are always crowded at Tough City, so be prepared to wait as the proprietor, a former carnival barker, regales patrons with colourful stories while his fast-moving staff whirl in a dervish of activity around him. Outdoor dining here on a mild Clayoquot evening will ensure picturesque memories, especially when the food is this good. You will find the traditional sushi favourites and West Coast originals like the prevailing favourite, the Dynamite Roll. You might also want to investigate the Spider Roll and the Crazy Ron Roll – the latter named in honour of the proprietor.

Entrée prices around $20; Sushi roll prices $5-$15.

BEER, WINE AND LIQUOR SALES

Government Liquor Store
328 Neill Street, beside the Common Loaf Bakery, 250-725-3722

Hundreds of varieties of beer, wine and ciders from around the world and a large collection of spirits.

Open: Monday-Saturday 10 am to 6 pm, Friday 10 am to 9 pm

Maquinna Cold Beer and Wine Shop
120 First Street at Main, 250-725-3261 extension 5

If you need it late, on Sunday or cold, the Cold Beer and Wine is the place to go. A smaller selection of beer, wine, cider and spirits than the Government Liquor Store (above) and slightly more expensive.

Open: 11 am until 11 pm, everyday

CATERING

If you need to feed an army, call in the specialists:

Breakers Deli (250-725-2558) can prepare box lunches, bulk salads and platters to go.

Wildside Grill (250-725-9453) caters by the plate with a sumptuous array of dishes.

SEAFOOD STORES

The Co-op Grocery Store
First Street at Campbell, 250-725-3226
Packaged local seafood, fresh wild salmon, halibut, sole, and scallops.

Crab Dock
Bottom of Olsen Road Drive 1.2 km from the Post Office out of town and turn left (east) on Olsen Road. The dock is 100 metres at the bottom of Olsen Road.

If your timing is good, you can get lucky and catch local fishermen just as they return with the day's haul. Transactions are cash only. Watch for signs on the highway: Jumbo Shrimp, Fresh Tuna, Local Halibut – you get the idea. It is worth driving down and asking at the dock even if you don't see any signs.

The Fish Store
366 Campbell Street, 250-725-2264
Fresh and cooked crab and a variety of fish are available seasonally. Ask about their exceptional smoking and packaging operation for your fresh-caught fish; an excellent way to preserve your catch for the trip home.

Scott's Fresh Crab
900 Campbell Street
Watch for the CRAB / OPEN sign across from the **Gas 'N Go / Long Beach Market**. Drive in and get fresh crab straight from the fisherman who hauled it up. Cash only. There is an Automatic Teller Machine (ATM) across the road at the gas station.

Trilogy Fish Company
634 Campbell Street, 250-725-2233, www.trilogyfish.net
Just next to the Weigh West Marina, specializing in fresh and smoked seafood products. Their Tofino Candied Salmon is drool-worthy. Hot and cold smoked salmon, fresh seafood, shellfish and live crab. Vacuum packaging service for your fresh fish ensures a safe trip home.

TOFINO GUIDE

Wildside Seafood
824 Ocean Park, 250-725-3244
This is hard to find but the quality of prawns and salmon make it worth the hunt. Drive 3.7 km towards Chesterman Beach from Tofino and turn left (east) on Hellesen Drive. Drive 200 metres and turn right at the end of the road. Go straight at the stop sign and watch for the Fresh Prawns and Salmon sign on your right, just past the children's park. It's best to call ahead before your visit to make sure that the proprietor is home.

FORAGING FOR TOFINO'S SEAFOOD

Fishing for, digging for and picking up crustaceans and other marine invertebrates is legal and rarely dangerous. Fishing for fin fish like coho salmon can be fun and productive, especially through August when they are abundant close to shore.

HOWEVER: Check the federal Department of Fisheries and Oceans office (DFO: 161 First Street at Campbell, 250-725-3500) for limits, edibility, and **licensing requirements** when harvesting your own seafood. Make sure you have whatever permit is required. Inform yourself if you could be in a shellfish harvesting region that has been flagged with **Red Tide** (p. 186). Understand that there are catch limits for each species of fin fish and shellfish and **it is irresponsible and illegal to harvest more than the legal limit**. The legal limits are printed in the free guide that you should pick up when you purchase your fishing license. You can also research limits at this DFO website: http://www.pac.dfo-mpo.gc.ca/fm-gp/rec/species-especes/shelltable-tableaucoquille-eng.htm.

PURCHASING A FISHING LICENSE
(Yes, you need this for shellfish, too!)

British Columbia separates the licensing of saltwater and freshwater fishing. Obviously, lake and river fishing requires a freshwater license. Fishing in the Pacific and harvesting shellfish requires a saltwater fishing license (also called a Tidal Water license).

Freshwater fishing licenses are only available for purchase online: www.fishing.gov.bc.ca

Saltwater fishing licenses are available online (www-ops2.pac.dfo-mpo.gc.ca/nrls-sndpp/index-eng.cfm) and at the following locations in Tofino:

TOFINO GUIDE

Co-op Hardware Store
121 First Street (at Main Street), 250-725-3436

Jay's Fly and Tackle Shop
561 Campbell Street, 888-534-7422 or 250-725-2700,
www.tofinofishing.com

Method Marine
380 Main Street on the pier, 250-725-3251,
www.methodmarine.com

CHECK FOR RED TIDE BEFORE HARVESTING SHELLFISH

Red Tide is a colloquialism for naturally occurring algal blooms that are poisonous to humans in high doses. Shellfish absorb the algae in high concentrations, so **it is very dangerous and potentially fatal to consume shellfish from an area that has a Red Tide**. The only way to know if an area is free of Red Tide is to check with authorities. Red Tide can be present in clear, uncoloured water.

Red Tide Closures for the Clayoquot and Tofino area are posted on this DFO website: www.pac.dfo-mpo.gc.ca/fm-gp/contamination/biotox/index-eng.htm and information is available by phone at DFO's Red Tide Hotline, 866-431-3474. Clayoquot Sound is Area 24. Be warned that the tables and maps on the website may be confusing if you are not familiar with the area, and there is significant risk in trying shellfish without knowing if the area is closed for Red Tide.

CAN I EAT THE MUSSELS?

YES! Two species of edible mussels can usually be harvested year round as long as you have a license. The blue mussel (*Mytilus edulis*) is the smaller species and the California mussel (*Mytilus californianus*) is the larger – both are delicious. Generally, mussels can be found on the rocks where there is heavy surf. Wait until low tide and then go picking with a paring knife. Choose medium size mussels and only those that are tightly closed. Clean by removing the beard and barnacles with a wire brush. Double check that you are harvesting mussels in an area free of Red Tide. **You must have a valid license to harvest mussels**. See above for more information about Red Tide and licensing.

WHERE CAN I FIND CLAMS IN CLAYOQUOT SOUND?

Although many different species of clams can be found at most beaches, they are most abundant on sandy or pebbly beaches near the tidal mudflats where there is a mix of fresh and salt water. Popular clamming spots are found on the tidal flats around Meares Island, although these are not easy to access. On any beach, look for the telltale holes in the muck or sand about the diameter of a pencil, and/or for heaps of open clam shells, previously pried open by other dextrous mammals. With one quick scoop of your shovel, dig down about 6 inches, turn over the shovel-full and pick out your clam.

Double check that you are harvesting clams in an area free of Red Tide. **You must have a valid license to harvest clams**. See above for more information about Red Tide and licensing.

> **Shellfish isn't supposed to be crunchy**
>
> Mussels and clams that soak in cold salt water with a half cup of raw oats overnight become sand free.

FINDING OYSTERS IN CLAYOQUOT SOUND

We have plenty of oysters in the area, but they are generally difficult for visitors to harvest. Don't worry if you can't find any, as Tofino's restaurants serve them in every way imaginable: deep fried, baked, barbequed and of course raw on the half shell. If the idea of slurping oysters is making you hungry, check out the annual Clayoquot Oyster Festival here in Tofino every November.

Lemmens Inlet is a commercial oyster growing area, with about a half dozen oyster farms, but harvesting oysters from farms without permission is of course illegal.

There are a few places in the Tofino area where oysters can be gathered on rocky shorelines, but finding these areas is difficult and requires boat access. If you do happen upon some oysters, make sure that they are the non-native Pacific oysters, because **the native Olympia oysters are protected under Canada's Species at Risk Act**. Olympia oysters are smaller and rounder than their Japanese cousins, the Pacific oysters. A good rule of thumb is to avoid harvesting oysters less than 6 centimetres in diameter. And do not forget to double check for a Red Tide closure in the area that you are harvesting.

WHAT ABOUT LIVE CRABS?

Without contest, Tofino's seafood scene is best known for its Dungeness crab (*Metacarcinus magister*). This sumptuously sweet crustacean is available at most restaurants in town or live from the seafood locations listed above, page 183. If you are buying live crab in Tofino with plans to cook it at your vacation rental or bed and breakfast, make sure that you have the proper facilities and ventilation to do so. Cooking crab indoors can stink something awful.

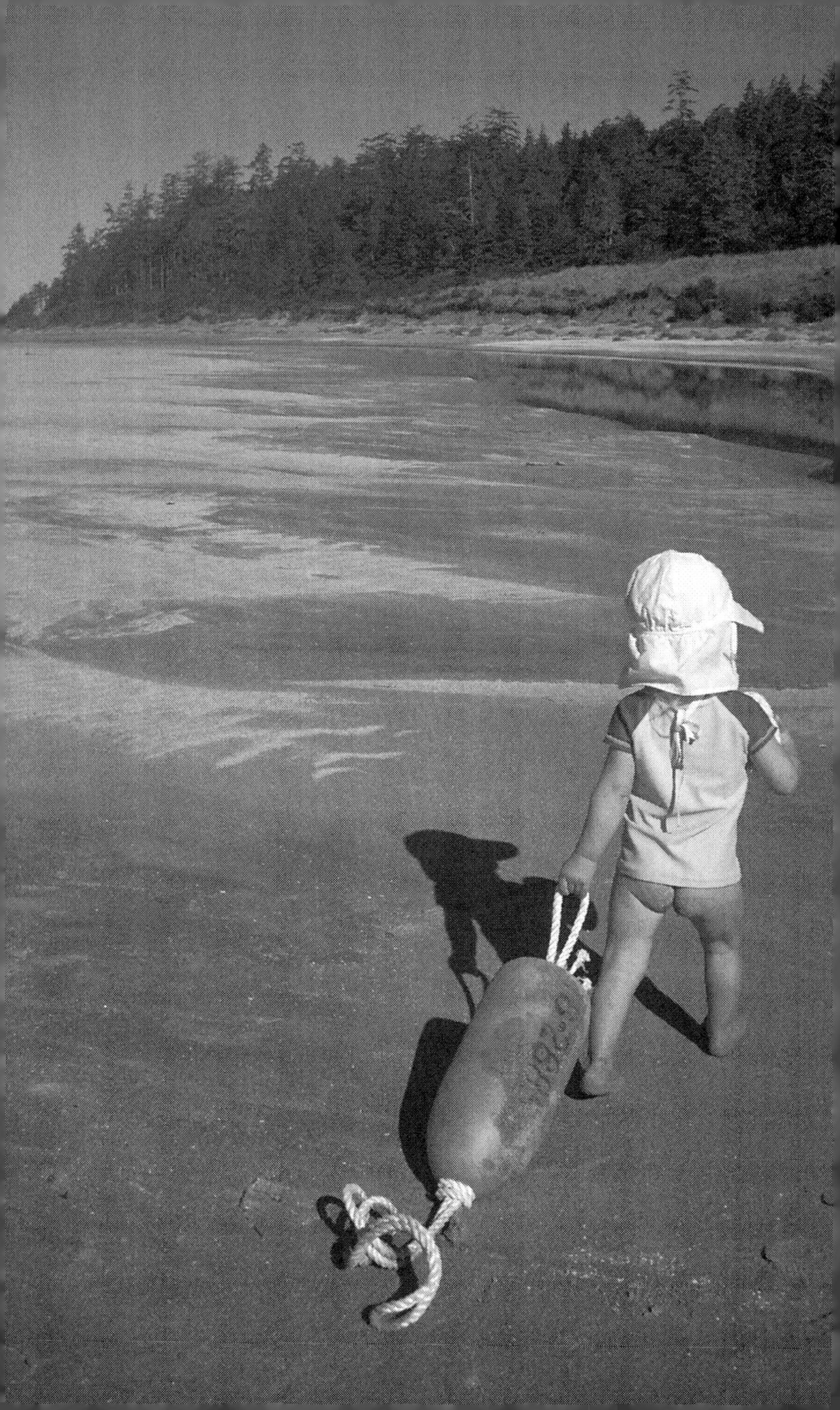

SHOPPING

Gifts and Souvenirs
Clothing and Outdoor Gear
Galleries and Studios
Groceries and Snacks
Bookstores
Public Market

GIFTS AND SOUVENIRS

Covet
368 Main Street, 250-725-2866, www.covettofino.com
Home accessories, hand-crafted furniture by local artisans, First Nations masks, candles, maritime items, baskets, clothing and jewellery. There is truly something for everyone here.

Driftwood Gift Shop
131 First Street at Campbell, 250-725-3905
Tofino's largest selection of souvenirs, sterling silver, souvenir clothing

Knits by the Sea
366 Campbell Street, 250-725-3700, www.knitsbythesea.com
Hand-spun and hand-dyed BC yarns and knitting supplies. A great spot to buy gifts for your knit-savvy friends and family.

Sandstone Jewellery and Gifts
346 Campbell Street at Second, 250-725-4482.
Good selection of traditional native arts, jewellery and an assortment of souvenirs and gifts.

Tofino Pharmacy
360 Campbell Street, 250-725-3101
Good postcard selection, local field guides, wide selection of Tofino-emblazoned clothing, boogie boards, largest art supply selection in Tofino.

Tree House Gift Company
305 Campbell Street at First, 250-725-4254
Tucked away and hard to see: next to the CIBC bank
Tofino souvenirs: tee shirts, sweatshirts, candles, frames, and other fine gifts. Also a good collection of regional books.

Wickaninnish Interpretive Centre
Wick Road, Pacific Rim National Park Reserve (p. 79 for directions)
Natural history books, stuffed animals, Canadian regalia, Parks-emblazoned clothing and other souvenirs and gifts.

YOU'RE IN GUMBOOT COUNTRY!

If you are planning on doing any beach walking in the fall, winter or spring months, it's best to bring or buy a good pair of *gumboots*. These tall, all-rubber boots are your best bet to keep your feet dry and warm on the beach. Long hikes in gumboots can cause painful blisters, though, so we recommend sturdy, high-top hiking boots with good soles for longer hikes on wet, slippery boardwalks and muddy trails.

Gumboot Tips
- **Wear thick socks inside your gumboots** to keep your feet cozy and comfortable. But be warned: socks inside gumboots can have a mind of their own, sliding down and inching their way off your feet. Experienced gumbooters outwit their socks, first tightly wrapping their pant legs around their ankles, and then hiking socks up as high as possible over pant legs. Taller socks with good elasticity come highly recommended.

- **Guard your boots from flooding.** Wet gumboots are difficult to dry and may remain damp for the rest of your vacation. To treat an unfortunate case of gumboot flooding, immediately prop the boot upside down as close to a heater or fireplace as is safely possible. A hairdryer can work in emergency situations.

- **Love your boots.** You will see many different colours, styles and heights of gumboots. Some boots may have buckles. Some may be pink and paisley. Fight the urge to run shamefacedly to the nearest clothing store to get the latest fashion. Embrace your black, yellow or orange beauties. Be proud, stand tall and love your inner-gumboot.

CLOTHING AND OUTDOOR GEAR

Bootique Upstairs
411 Campbell Street, 250.725-2136
A "funky lifestyle boutique" located above and behind The Whale Centre (p. 87). Specializes in women's clothing, lingerie, jewellery.

Co-op Hardware Store
121 First Street at Main 250-725-3436
Our main hardware store. Also carries camping gear, auto supplies, marine charts, printer cartridges, kitchen supplies, garden supplies.

Family Fashions Clothing Store
341 Campbell Street at Second, 250-725-4227
Great for inexpensive gumboots, flip flops and rain gear. Full selection of men's, women's and children's clothing and footwear.

Rod's Power and Marine
591Campbell Street, 250-725-3735
Marine equipment and repairs. Chainsaws and some logging supplies

Storm Light Marine Station
380 Main, 250-725-3342, www.stormlightoutfitters.com
A good and varied selection of outdoor gear, marine supplies and camping gear.
Brand names like Columbia, Outdoor Research, MSR and others. Check out the discount room in the back for excellent deals.

Studio House & Project Monster Studios
451Main Street, 250-725-8811, www.projectmonster.ca
A combination of artful, mostly women's clothing and eye-catching paintings by local artist, Julie Robinson. An eclectic and fun place to browse.

Tofino DNA
411 Main Street, 250-725-3316
Locally printed hooded sweatshirts and tee shirts made from alternative materials like hemp, bamboo, organic cotton. Also a large selection of jewellery.

Tofino Fishing and Trading Co.
120 Fourth Street at Campbell 250-725-2622,
www.tofinofishingandtrading.com
High-end outdoor accessories, raingear, charts, maps, ship's brass.
Brand names like Royal Robbins, Merrell, Timberland, North Face and others. Best bet for a quality pair of hiking boots.

Tofino Sea Kayaking Company
320 Main Street, 250-725-4222, www.tofino-kayaking.com
High-end sea kayaking gear, and marine-oriented backcountry camping supplies.

Tuff Kids
381 Main Street, 250-725-3290, www.tuffkids.ca
At the back of the building, facing Campbell Street
Toys, children's clothing and accessories for sale. Also rents playpens, cribs, child carrying backpacks, baby gates, highchairs, and strollers.

TOFINO GUIDE

What to do if you see a...

COUGAR

Give thanks to the wildlife gods: you are one of the few people to have seen the most elusive and arguably the most attractive land mammal in British Columbia.

Cougars (*Puma concolor*) are fierce predators, known to kill moose that are over 270 kg (600 pounds!). You are more likely to be killed by lightning than a cougar, so do not be afraid of hiking and exploring while you are on your vacation. In the last 100 years there have only been 6 recorded deaths from cougar attacks in British Columbia. But the animals are here, and you should always exercise caution when you are in or at the edge of a wilderness area.

Never leave children unattended, and **be particularly cautious in the early morning, evening and at night**. If you have the rare opportunity of seeing a cougar, stay calm, stand tall and look directly at the animal while you back away slowly. If it does not show signs of fear, or seems threatening, do not run away as your instinct will suggest; be large, aggressive and loud in order to show him or her that you are not an easy meal. Continue to back away while looking straight at the animal.

See page 121 for more information about cougar encounters.

GALLERIES AND STUDIOS

Clayoquot Crafts
671 Industrial Way, 250-725-3990, www.clayoquotcrafts.com
Hand crafted furniture made from clear western red cedar for your home and garden. Collapsible designs make the pieces easy to take home. Exceptional quality of workmanship and materials make this workshop well worth a visit.

Eagle Aerie Gallery of Roy H. Vickers
350 Campbell Street at Second, 250-725-3235 or 800-663-0669, www.royhenryvickers.com
In the form of a traditional longhouse, this gallery has originals and print works by the artist in a spectacular setting. Roy is one of British Columbia's most celebrated artists. His work has been presented to Queen Elizabeth II, Boris Yeltsin and Bill Clinton and his art is featured in the Canadian Museum of Civilization.

Elements Pottery Studio
268 First Street, 250-725-3964
West Coast inspired pottery pieces and art plaques by Cathy White. The studio is open when the sign is out, or by appointment.

House of Himwitsa
300 Main Street at First, 250-725-2017, www.himwitsa.com
Large First Nations gallery filled with masks, basketry, prints and jewellery.

Keith Plumley Studio
1180 Pacific Rim Highway, 250-726-5098,
www.tofinoartworks.net
Located in the Live to Surf parking lot, these artistic expressions in British Columbia's native woods include 2-metre wide wood turnings

TOFINO GUIDE

Reflecting Spirit Gallery
411 Campbell Street at Third 250-725-2472, www.reflectingspirit.ca
Wide selection from local artists including photographs, paintings, masks, sculpture, pottery and jewellery. Located above the **Whale Centre**

Shorewinds Gallery
120 Fourth Street at Campbell 250-725-1222, www.shorewindgallery.com
Features local artist **Mark Hobson** and other others from around the West Coast. Also a selection of jewellery, pottery, sculpture and weaving.

Solart Glass Studio
Live to Surf parking lot, 250-725-3122, www.solmaya.com
Handblown glass pieces by Sol Maya are displayed for sale and often forged by the artist right in front of your eyes in the on-site kiln.

Tofino Art Glass Studio
264 First Street, 250-725-3929, www.tofinoartglass.com
Kevin Midgley's elite glassworks with West Coast designs. Glass plates and trays, pendants, bowls, masks and other assorted glass art pieces.

Tofino Botanical Gardens
1084 Pacific Rim Highway, 250-725-1220, www.tbgf.org
Put simply: If you like large sculpture, you should visit these gardens. Some of the outbuildings, like Jan Janzen's gazebo at the pond, qualify as works of art. See page 207 for more information.

Village Gallery
321 Main Street, 250-725-4229
A wide range of fine art. Pottery, soapstone carvings, jewellery, distinctive gifts.

GROCERIES AND SNACKS

Beaches Grocery
1184 Pacific Rim Highway in the Live to Surf parking lot,
250-725-2270
A truly convenient convenience store in the beaches area catering to all sorts of appetites and needs. Great cheeses and pre-packaged sandwiches. Good baguettes and a varied selection of frozen meats and fish, kept in the back. Just ask.

Blends for Friends
181 Fourth Street, 250-725-4283
Hours vary – phone or stop by for more information
Bulk foods, herbs and spices. Also essential oils and crystals.

Co-op Convenience Store (at Co-op Gas Bar)
797 Campbell Street, 250-725-3225
Open 7 days a week: 6 am – 10 pm
Munchies, coffee, newspapers – typical gas station fare

Co-op Grocery Store
First Street at Campbell at Campbell, 250-725-3226
Open 7 days a week: 8:30 am to 9 pm
Tofino's largest grocery store, everyone in town goes there

Green Soul Organics
Fourth Street at Campbell, 250-725-4202,
www.greensoulorganics.com
Open 7 days a week: 10 am to 9 pm
Tofino's natural foods grocery store. A good selection of organic produce, some organic meats, local and regional products, and lots of yummy natural food snacks.

L.A. Grocery/Convenience
131 First Street at Campbell, 250-725-4251
Open 7 days a week: 8 am to 11 pm
Stocks the basic food groups and is open late: newspapers, munchies, good magazine selection, ATM, beach toys and movie rentals.

TOFINO GUIDE

Long Beach Market (at the Gas 'N Go)
921 Campbell Street, 250-725-2050
Open 7 days a week: 6:30 am to 10:30 pm
Snacks, treats, good ice cream selection, firewood and some camping supplies

Six Hundred Degrees Baking
250-725-3933, www.sixhundreddegrees.com
Exceptional artisan breads and treats baked with organic ingredients in a wood-fired oven. Reliably available on Saturdays at the Public Market (p. 201). Get a cinnamon bun if you can -- they sell out quickly! A variety of breads from Six Hundred Degrees are also available at Beaches Grocery (above) and SOBO (p. 179).

BOOKSTORES

Mermaid Tales Bookshop
465 Campbell Street (beside the downtown Visitor Centre), 250-725-2125, www. mermaidbooks.ca
Tofino's largest bookstore. Focused on "meaningful and intelligent writing," but also carries bestsellers and good beach reading too. Provides a great selection of kites and quirky toys for kids and playful adults.

Wildside Books & Espresso Bar (located in the Tofino Sea Kayaking Company building)
320 Main Street, 250-725-4222, www.tofino-kayaking.com
Features local, regional and international authors, as well as travel and nature guidebooks
Good espresso coffee and a great view from their waterfront deck.

PUBLIC MARKET

Vendors include local artisans, home bakers, market gardeners, and wild food harvesters, all of whom must "make it, bake it, grow it, gather it" in order to participate in this festive Saturday market.

Residents and visitors enjoy visiting the market to browse, shop and play at the skatepark and children's play area. Music and cart-served food add to the festive atmosphere.

Every Saturday, May through October 10 pm to 2 pm at the **Tofino Village Green**, located between Second and Third Streets on Campbell.

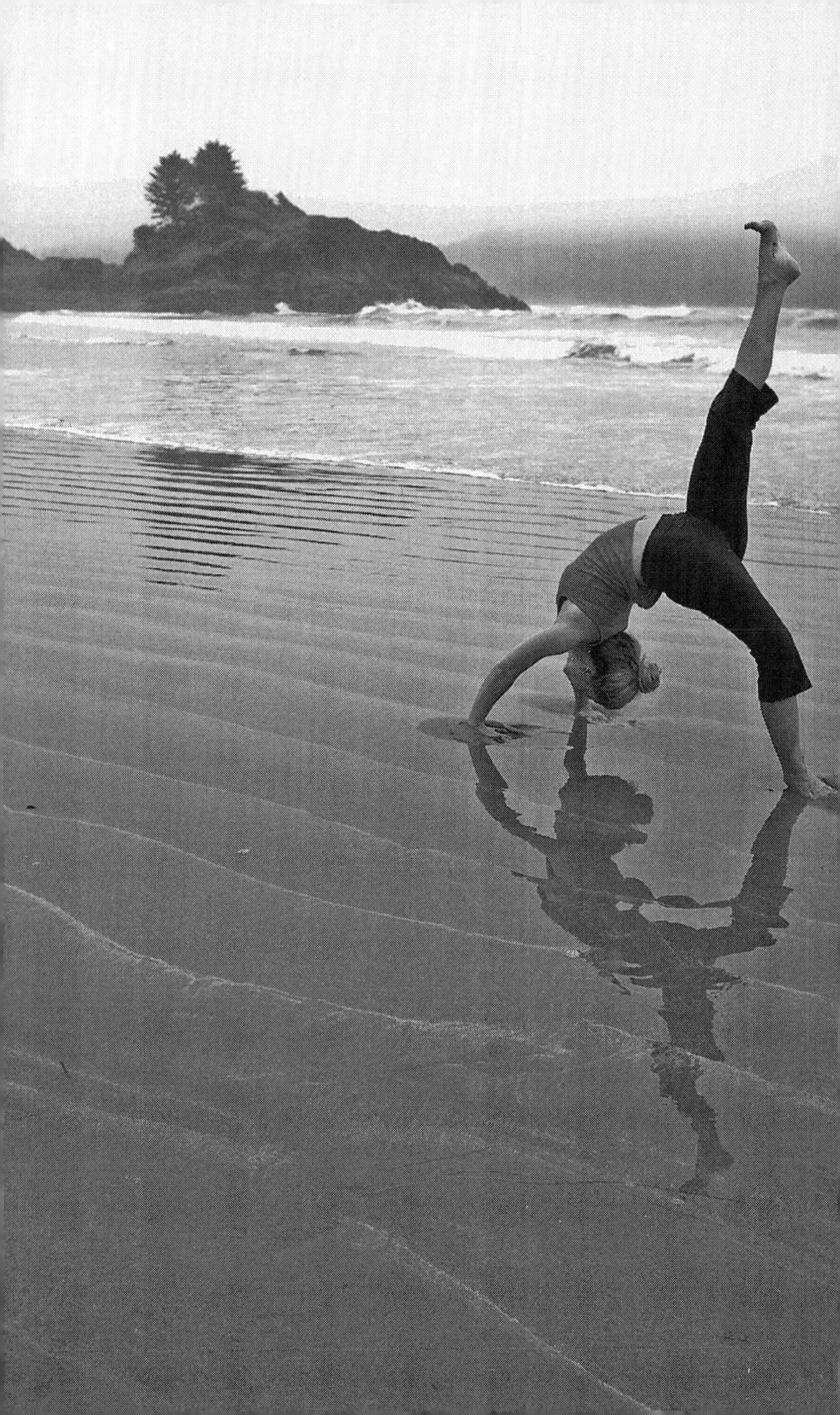

FITNESS & LEISURE

Spas, Yoga, Body & Hair Care

Gardens: Private and Public

Running and Jogging

Multi-Use Path (MUP)

Bicycle Rentals & Services

Salt Water Swimming

Fresh Water Swimming

Indoor Pools

Skatepark, Tennis, Basketball

Golfing and Mini Golf

Kite Flying and Kiteboarding

Rock Climbing

Top 10 Things to do in Tofino with the Kids

TOFINO GUIDE

SPAS, YOGA, BODY & HAIR CARE

Affinity Massage Studio
230 Fourth Street, 250-725-2072,
www.affinitymassagestudio.com

A range of treatments are available including Shiatsu, deep flow and hot stone massage.

Ancient Cedars Spa at Wickaninnish Inn
Osprey Lane, 250-725-3100, www.wickinn.com

The spa at the Wickaninnish Inn offers a variety of different body treatments for guests, visitors and residents. Among their offerings: a soothing aromatic massage, rejuvenating thalassotherapy treatment, Jin Shin Do, and reflexology. If you are really stressed out, try the detoxifying body wrap with seaweed, juniper, rosemary, thyme and lavender. An impressive **steam room** is located on-site. Individual steams may be booked in advance even if you are not a guest at the inn. Phone for details.

Arbutus Health Centre
1180 Pacific Rim Highway (Live to Surf parking lot), 250-725-2212, www.arbutushealth.com

Offers acupuncture, counselling, massage therapy and private yoga from a team of practitioners.

Ashram Spa at Cable Cove Inn
201 Main Street, 800-663-6449 or 250-725-4236,
www.cablecoveinn.com

The spa has a menu of body therapy and massage options to choose from including a Milk and Honey Body Buff, Shiatsu, a variety of massage therapies including hot stone. Yoga classes are taught in a yurt located on the property. Find Cable Cove at the terminus of Main Street by continuing through the last stop sign at First Street. This may be the furthest west you can drive on a paved road in Canada.

Coastal Bliss Yoga
1180 Pacific Rim Highway (Live to Surf parking lot),
www.coastalblissyoga.com

Tofino's only studio dedicated to yoga. Offers a variety of yoga classes daily. See the studio's website or stop by for scheduling information.

Sacred Stone Wellness Studio
421 Main Street, 250-725-3341, www.sacredstone.ca

A full spa with multiple treatment rooms, Sacred Stone offers an array of body therapies and wellness-based aesthetic services, hot stone massage and Ayurveda treatments. The spa recently added an infrared sauna and sells a variety of body therapy oils and creams.

Sacred Presence Energy Balancing Therapies
680 Ocean Park Avenue, 250-725-2820, www.reflectingspirit.ca

Lomi-lomi massage and hot stone massage from a certified Eden Energy Medicine practitioner.

Salty Dolls Hair Salon
381 Main Street, 250-266-0266, www.saltydollshairsalon.com

Women and Men's hair cutting, colouring, perms and straightening.

Studio One
1180 Pacific Rim Highway (Live to Surf parking lot),
250-725-3450, www.studioonetofino.ca

Aveda Concept Salon with women and men's hair cutting, colouring, perms, straightening. Also offers some spa services: facials, waxing, make up, tinting, manicures and pedicures.

TOFINO GUIDE

Therese Bouchard
South Chesterman Road, 250-725-4278

Certified in massage therapy with over 20 years experience. Therese is also a Trager Practitioner and a clinical hypno-therapist. Her studio is located in a West Coast architectural delight. Call for an appointment.

GARDENS: PRIVATE AND PUBLIC

Tofino Botanical Gardens
1084 Pacific Rim Highway, 250-725-1220, www.tbgf.org
Five hectares of gardens, forest and shoreline. The gardens opened in 1997 as a place to explore the relationship between culture and nature in Clayoquot Sound. A network of paths and boardwalks meander through the forest and down to Tofino's otherwise inaccessible mudflats. Wander from the garden's visitor centre past kitchen gardens, the Frog Pond and the Children's Garden into the lush old growth rainforest. The garden's field guide is a must-read while you admire the impressive collection of native and non-native plants. The outdoor sculpture and interpretive art installations at the Tofino Botanical Gardens are whimsical and thought provoking. Well worth at least an afternoon.

Open to the public by admission: Adults, $11; Students, $6.50; Children 12 and under, free. Admission is for three days, so you can come back for more.

Ken Gibson's Rhododendron Hill, Fourth Street at Gibson
As you pull up to the stop sign at Fourth Street, look west (away from the harbour) and up, way up. Perched on a hill overlooking Tofino, Ken Gibson has spent more than 30 years collecting and planting over 1000 varieties of rhododendrons. Ken has been called "Canada's Recognized Rhodo Ambassador" by the American Rhododendron Society. The blooms start in early spring and peak in early summer. This iconic setting has been displayed on numerous post cards of Tofino.

Private garden, but polite viewing from the edges is encouraged.

Stubbs Island Gardens, Stubbs Island
Long before Tofino existed, the original trading settlement in Clayoquot Sound was on Stubbs Island, about 1.5 km offshore from the First Street dock. Stubbs Island has extensive gardens, parts of which date back to fur-trading days, when the store, hotel,

saloon and post office here were the hub of local activity. The island is now a **private nature preserve**, and talented caretakers lovingly maintain the many hectares of garden. Enhanced and expanded over the years, the gardens on Stubbs Island are **open to the public for one magical weekend every year, the Victoria Day weekend in late May**. Boat transportation is generously provided for this event at no cost, and hundreds of people make the trip across the water to marvel at these gardens and to picnic on the island's sandy beaches and manicured lawns.

What to do if you see a...

STELLER'S JAY

Don't shoot! If you are familiar with the jay family of birds, you will recognize this dark iridescent blue, robin-sized, crested beauty. The Steller's jay (*Cyanocitta stelleri*) is loved by visitors for its looks and bravado, but scorned by resident gardeners for its clever ability to find and steal every seed and newly sprouted plant on their property. The legendary coastal gardener, **Cougar Annie** (see below), was rumoured to have a three-part solution to this pest problem: trapping, boiling and eating. Regardless of their errant ways, Steller's jays are a delight to watch, particularly if you get to witness their raucous and sometimes scornful calls.

Freedom Cove Floating Garden, Cypress Bay, Clayoquot Sound

This series of floating gardens and sculptures on docks attached to the owners' float home has been featured in Canadian Geographic and "Weird Homes" TV Show. Freedom Cove is a remote location, only accessible by boat or float plane. The gardens are open to the public by tour. The departure times and length of the tour varies, depending on demand, weather and your group's needs. There is a video online, showing the gardens: www.youtube.com/watch?v=DDqbfiejLdM. Phone **Browning Pass Charters** (250-725-3342, www.browningpass.com) for more information.

Cougar Annie's Garden, Boat Basin, Clayoquot Sound

A remote heritage garden dating back to 1915. The five-acre garden was created out of the dense forest by Ada (Annie) Rae-Arthur who sold mail-order plants from her nursery garden and ran a small store and post office on her 117 acre homestead. She became renowned as a cougar hunter, killing over seventy in her lifetime. She stayed in her remote garden for nearly 70 years, rarely leaving. She bore eight of her eleven children there, outlived and outworked four husbands, and by the time she died in 1985 she was already a coastal legend.

Peter Buckland single-handedly resurrected the garden -- mostly with a chainsaw -- after it had been neglected for years. Peter subsequently created the **Boat Basin Foundation** for the property in order to "maintain and preserve Cougar Annie's garden for future generations, and to encourage education in temperate rainforest ecology." Margaret Horsfield's book *Cougar Annie's Garden* tells the story of this compelling place.

Commercial fly-in tours of the garden are possible, also pre-arranged boat visits. Allow a full day for a trip here; it is 55 kilometres north of Tofino and very remote.

Contact the **Boat Basin Foundation** for more information: www.boatbasin.org.

TOFINO GUIDE

RUNNING AND JOGGING

In 1999, we began hosting our own official West Coast marathon, the **Edge to Edge Marathon**. Since then, we have seen an increased number of Tofino residents in training, pounding the pavement and beaches. Tofino runners continue to do well in this event, despite the increasing awareness of this race on the marathon circuit.

A good **10 km run** starts in town at the Village Green (Third and Campbell Street). Jog south along the highway. Just before the **Gas 'N Go** (1.5 km), you can jump onto the **Multi-Use Path** (p. 219) paralleling the highway on your left (east). Run for a further 2.5 km south and carefully cross the highway at Lynn Road. Staying on the road surface, veer left onto Chesterman Beach Road when you reach the Y at Osprey Lane. Alternatively, you can detour and run the same stretch on the beach by going through the parking area in front of you and down the 100 metre path through a giant Sitka spruce grove and onto **North Chesterman Beach** (p. 66).

If you choose to run along the beach here, after about 1.5 km watch for a public path up to Chesterman Beach Road on your left, about 400 metres before you get to the rocky dead-end. Take this public access trail back to ***Chesterman Beach Road*** *and turn right.*

If you choose to stay on the road, jog about 1.5 km and connect with the highway and Multi-Use Path.

Cross the highway and turn back (left) toward downtown. The 10 km mark puts you at the **Gas 'N Go**. From there you can walk a 1.5 km cool-down past the **Eik Cedar Tree** (p. 45) and back to town.

Of course the most popular place for a good run is the beach. For a good 5 km return-circuit, get out to **Chesterman Beach** at low tide and jog the entire beach, including Frank Island. For an extended beach run we suggest **Long Beach** (p. 130), but remember you'll have to be able to make it back to your car; be responsible about turning around for the return trip.

MULTI-USE PATH (MUP)

The Multi-Use Path is a 2-metre wide paved trail that follows along the edge of the east side of the highway for about 6 km. The MUP begins just north of **Long Beach Market / Gas 'N Go** and continues for 5.8 km to the Cox Bay Visitor Centre (p. 27). Cyclists, walkers, leashed dogs and joggers are all welcome to use the MUP. It is possible to cycle the entire 7.5 km from the downtown core of Tofino to the Cox Bay Visitor Centre but be warned that there are a few dangerous sections of the MUP where there is only a narrow strip of gravel alongside the highway.

TOFINO GUIDE

BICYCLE RENTALS & SERVICES

The MUP (p. 219) provides an excellent cycling conduit from locations along the highway to Chesterman Beach and Cox Bay. Riding bicycles on the beaches is perfectly legal and very fun, but note that some bike rental companies (see below) prohibit beach riding because of the excessive wear and salt corrosion on the bikes.

The MUP ends at Cox Bay, and some visitors choose to cycle further to Long Beach. This is legal, and potentially fun, but **cycling along the edge of the Pacific Rim Highway can be extremely dangerous**. Vehicle traffic is constant in July and August, and there is very little space along the edge of the highway, between the traffic on your left and the steep ditch on your right. Only attempt this trip if you are a confident cyclist and have experienced narrow highway shoulders in heavy highway traffic.

Groovy Movie, 1180 Pacific Rim Highway, 250-725-2722

Rents beach cruiser bicycles from inside the movie store. Located in the Live to Surf parking lot.

TOF Cycles, 660 Sharp Road, 250-725-2453

"Bicycle Mark" runs this go-to bike repair shop in Tofino. A variety of bike rentals and sales on-site.

SALT WATER SWIMMING

There are kilometres upon kilometres of beaches to choose from. The local favourite is Chesterman Beach on a calm day. Wear a wetsuit (rentals available: p. 106) or be very aware of how long you are in the water: it is dangerous to become over-chilled and these waters are... chilly. If you are swimming close to shore, be very mindful of currents, tides, swell height and weather conditions. Strong currents and unexpected or rogue waves can really shake you up, especially in the winter months.

FRESH WATER SWIMMING

The closest, most accessible lake for swimming is Kennedy Lake. The water temperatures vary during the year but can always be guaranteed to be warmer than the Pacific. This area is usually sunny during Tofino's sometimes foggy August days, making it a popular destination for residents when the fog in Tofino persists.

You can access a shallow, sandy beach at Kennedy Lake by starting at the **Visitor Centre at The Junction** (p. 26) and driving 5.9 km northwest (back towards Port Alberni) to a narrow gravel road on your left. Slow down, the road is easy to miss. Turn down this road and drive about 400 metres to a parking area. This is a narrow arm of the Pacific Rim National Park Reserve. At the parking area you will see a composting toilet facility and a trail down to the sandy beach. Swimmers Itch can be present in the shallow waters at this beach, so you would be wise to ask someone at the beach if he or she is familiar with the present conditions. Swimmers Itch, common in some British Columbia lakes, is caused by a harmless but annoying parasite that creates itchy red spots or bumps on the skin. The bumps go away after a few days or a week.

INDOOR POOLS

There are two indoor swimming pools with hot tubs **open to the public**.

The pool facility at **MacKenzie Beach Resort** (p. 224) is open 7 days a week, 10:00 am to 8:00 pm. Drive 3.3 km south from the Post Office and turn right (west) on MacKenzie Beach Road. Drive about 600 metres and turn into the MacKenzie Beach Resort. Go to the office and pay about $5 for access to the pool facilities, collect your key and get directions to the building where the pool is located.

The pool facility at **Ocean Village Beach Resort** (p. 224) is open Sundays, Tuesdays and Thursdays 3:00 to 6:00 pm. Drive 3.6 km south from the Post Office and turn right (west) on Hellesen Drive. Continue about 300 metres down Hellesen and turn right at the Ocean Village sign just before the beach parking area. Pay about $5 at the office and get the combination to the lock on the dressing rooms for access.

SKATEPARK, TENNIS, BASKETBALL

Find all of these activities freely available at the Village Green, between Second and Third Streets on Campbell. The **Tofino Skatepark** is a well designed, safe and fun skateboarding area. There are two good public asphalt tennis courts and a decent basketball court above the skatepark in the chain link fenced area.

GOLFING AND MINI GOLF

Long Beach Golf Course and Campground is located on Pacific Rim Highway, 14 km south of Tofino within the Pacific Rim National Park Reserve boundaries. This is a challenging nine-hole course with play straight through the rainforest. The relaxed and approachable staff at the fully stocked pro shop rent all necessary equipment including power and pull carts. Friendly and professional instruction is also available if you would like to perfect your wayward swing. The **Back Nine Bar and Grill** (p. 168) is open seasonally for breakfast, lunch, dinner, and snacks. Expect to pay about $25 for nine holes or about $35 for an 18 hole game.

The campground (p. 237) has 76 campsites for tents or RVs.

Long Beach Golf Course also has an 18-hole **mini golf course and a driving range** on-site.

Long Beach Golf Course
1850 Pacific Rim Highway, 250-725-3332,
www.longbeachgolfcourse.com

Turn left on Grice Road at the Golf Course/Camping sign about 14 km south of the Post Office on the Pacific Rim Highway. Turn right in ten metres at the sign.

KITE FLYING AND KITEBOARDING

The prevailing ocean breezes will almost certainly guarantee lift. So if you can't fly your kite here, the problem isn't the kite.

For traditional **kite flying**, set up at the middle portion of Chesterman Beach (p. 66) on most sunny summer days.

Kiteboarding is a relatively new sport that combines flying a large kite with surfing the ocean swells on a small board. Kiteboarders usually set up at the middle portion of Chesterman Beach, and then snug up to the south side (left) of Frank Island on Chesterman Beach, accessed from the middle parking lot.

You will find kites at:

Driftwood
First Street at Campbell, 250-725-3905

L A Grocery
131 First Street, 250-725-4251

Mermaid Tales Bookstore
465 Campbell Street, 250-725-2125, www.mermaidtales.ca

Tofino Pharmacy
360 Campbell Street, 250-725-3101

Long Beach Market at the Gas 'N Go
921 Campbell Street, 250-725-2050

ROCK CLIMBING

The Alternative: Tofino's Indoor Climbing Gym
681 Industrial Way (unit B), 250-725-8777, www. climbtofino.com

The climbing gym is a welcome physical activity on a rainy day. The walls are 10 metres high with top ropes anchored in place and belay devices provided. There is plenty of room for bouldering in the cave. All gear rentals and instruction are available.

TOP 10 THINGS TO DO IN TOFINO WITH THE KIDS

1. Check out the displays at the Wickaninnish Interpretive Centre

2. Attend a Parks presentation at Green Point Campground's Theatre

3. Visit the Whale Centre Museum

4. Roast wieners and marshmallows, build sandcastles, fly a kite. All to be done at the beach.

5. Rent boogie boards and wet suits to hit the waves, or visit Tofino's Skatepark

6. Take the family kayaking with a guide

7. Head to the Raincoast Interpretive Centre to find fun outdoor education activities

8. Observe Tidal Pools at Chesterman's Beach or MacKenzie Beach (low tide required)

9. Visit the Playground at the Village Green (between Second and Third Streets on Campbell Street).

10. Shop for great children's books, games or toys at one of the local gift stores

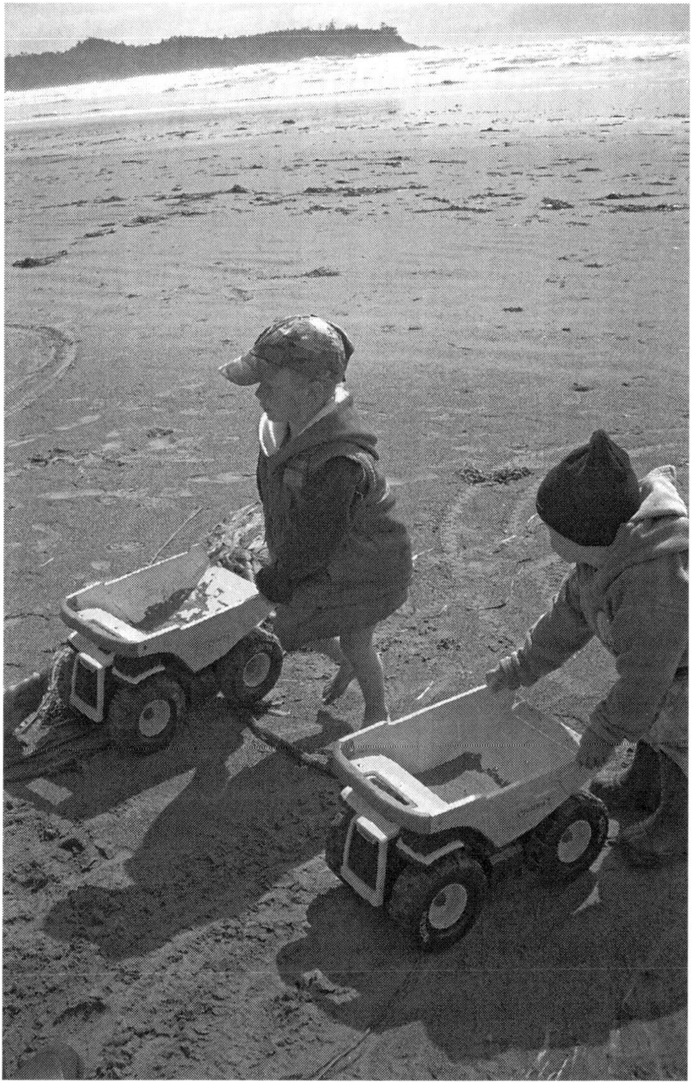

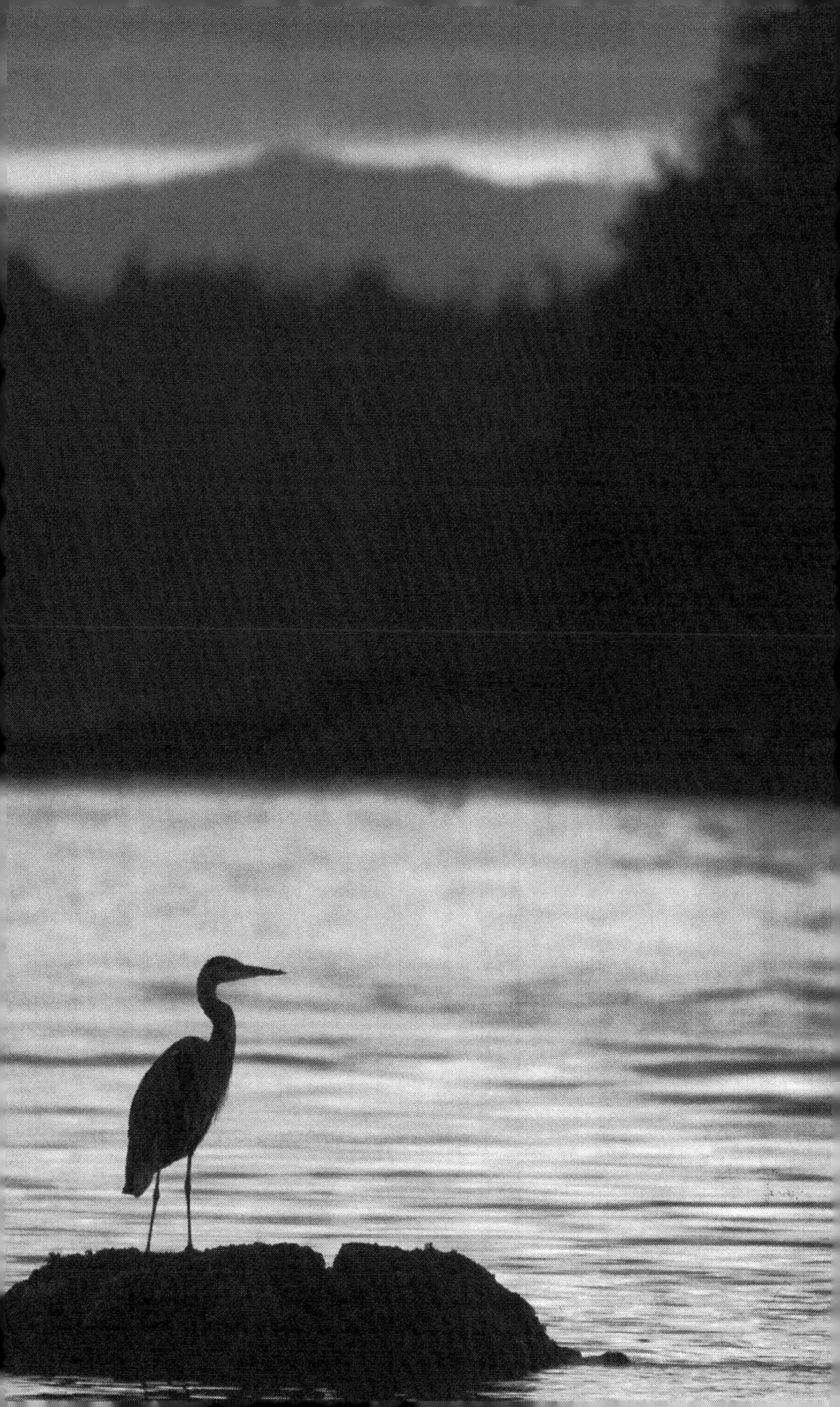

ACCOMMODATION LISTINGS

Reservations and Rates

Beachfront Resorts, Lodges and Hotels

Hotels, Motels, and Resorts (not on the beach)

Bed and Breakfasts & Vacation Rentals

Hostels

Accommodation at Hot Springs Cove

Campgrounds

Glamping: Glamorous Camping

TOFINO GUIDE

RESERVATIONS AND RATES

We cannot stress enough that **planning ahead is very important** if you are visiting Tofino in the peak tourism season (mid June to early September). People who fail to book ahead sometimes have to turn around and drive 2 hours back to Port Alberni in the dark because they thought that Tofino was still the quaint little fishing village they visited in 1969. It isn't. Times have changed and Tofino is one of the most popular tourist destinations in Canada. **Accommodations, including campsites, book up a long time in advance**. Vacancies can be difficult to find between mid June and September, so we urge you to make your reservation for accommodations well in advance.

The rates for accommodations in Tofino vary with the seasons. Most accommodation providers have two or three different seasonal rates. Summer (mid June to early September) is the most expensive time in Tofino and most accommodation providers require at least a three-night minimum during this peak season. **A rough list of summer rates follows.** You may find a few places either less or more expensive; **these rates are approximate**.

- $200 to $700 per night at a beach resort
- $200 to $700 per night for a vacation rental home or cottage
- $150 to $300 per night at a bed and breakfast
- $150 to $250 per night at a hotel or motel
- $40 to $60 per night for a campsite
- $30 to $40 per night at a hostel

Generally, the closer you are to a beach, the more expensive the accommodation.

Fall, winter or early spring vacations in Tofino can be surprisingly affordable. Accommodation providers discount their rates significantly during these seasons, especially if you avoid weekends. For example, some beach resorts may have $90 per night specials in December and January for the same room that could cost upwards of $350 per night in the summer. In the thick of winter you should be able to find a decent motel room for around $60 per night.

BEACHFRONT RESORTS, LODGES AND HOTELS

This section of our accommodation list provides information about large resorts with hotel-style accommodation and/or self-contained cabins for rent on beachfront properties. Smaller beachfront accommodations are listed in the **Bed and Breakfasts and Vacation Rentals** category below. A few large harbour-front hotels are listed in the **Hotels, Motels and Resorts (not on the beach)** section.

All venues in the following lists are in geographic order from south to north.

On Cox Bay

Cox Bay Beach Resort
1431 Pacific Rim Highway, 250-725-2600,
www.coxbaybeachresort.com

Two rows of self-contained, independently owned beach homes are connected by covered, elevated boardwalks and professionally administered by an on-site management team. This narrow property is home to 20 one-bedroom suites and 20 two-bedroom suites nestled into a well landscaped, intimate setting. All guests have access to the sauna and the outdoor hot tub overlooking the beach. Each suite has a fully equipped kitchen, deck and fireplace. The resort is on the waterfront of Cox Bay, providing direct access to this popular summer surfing location.

Long Beach Lodge Resort
1441 Pacific Rim Highway, 877-844-7873 or 250-725-2442,
www.longbeachlodgeresort.com

The main lodge houses 41 splendid rooms, some of which are perched right over the sand on majestic Cox Bay. The 8-acre property also has 20 two-bedroom cottages tastefully lined up along the driveway into the main lodge. The cottages are attractive and well kept. Each cottage has a gas fireplace in the living room, a full kitchen, two bathrooms and a fenced patio with a hot tub. The Lodge's on-site restaurant (p. 176) is fantastic.

Pacific Sands Resort
1421 Pacific Rim Highway, 800-565-2322 or 250-725-3322, www.pacificsands.com

Tofino's original beach resort lies at the northern corner of Cox Bay on a huge grassy property leading down to the sand. The resort is big, but multiple well-designed buildings keep the atmosphere cozy: 5 different buildings have one and two-bedroom self contained suites and there are 22 luxury villas where you can choose from a one, two or three-bedroom configuration. With so many different options comes a long and inviting list of amenities: hot tubs, beachfront suites, patios over the ocean, suites that open onto the lawn, BBQs, indoor fireplaces. Pacific Sands has been providing friendly, family-oriented beachfront accommodation with exceptional reviews since 1972.

On Chesterman Beach
Wickaninnish Inn
Osprey Lane, 800-333-4604 or 250-725-3100, www.wickinn.com

In a 2010 report on the "Top 50 Resorts in the US and Canada", the magazine *Travel + Leisure* rated the Wickaninnish Inn #4, taking the report's highest marks for all of Canada. Two separate hotel buildings are located at the very north end of Chesterman Beach. The Wickaninnish-at-the-Point has 45 rooms perched on a spectacular rocky headland and the Wickaninnish-on-the-Beach has 12 suites and 18 rooms located right on Chesterman Beach. Both buildings are filled with artistic marvels in their structure and decor. Access to the in-house Ancient Cedars Spa (p. 204) and the upscale restaurant, The Pointe (p. 177), make "The Wick" a favourite destination for those who seek the extra luxuries in life.

TOFINO GUIDE

On MacKenzie Beach

Crystal Cove Beach Resort
1165 Cedarwood Place, 250-725-4213,
www.crystalcovebeachresort.com

Over 30 splendid small log cabins situated along the beach, in the forest and *in the trees*. Yes, really! The treehouse cabins are a favourite for kids. Exceptionally manicured grounds with a full playground accentuate the family-friendly nature of this resort. Also home to over 70 serviced RV sites (p. 237).

Ocean Village Beach Resort
At the end of Hellesen Drive, 866-725-3755 or 250-725-3755,
www.oceanvillageresort.com

One and two-bedroom single cottages right on the beach as well as smaller studio cottages standing between 15 and 30 metres from the beach. The grounds consist of an expansive and welcoming lawn, seamlessly connecting to the beach. Indoor pool and hot tub.

Tin Wis Best Western Resort
1119 Pacific Rim Highway, 800-661-9995 or 250-725-4445,
www.tinwis.com

A three-storey hotel with 85 oceanfront rooms, about 75 steps away from the beach, across the lawn. The in-house restaurant (p. 180) serves a great breakfast and dinner. **This is Tofino's only conference/convention centre**, with a large meeting hall equipped for groups of up to 250 people. Owned and operated by the Tla-o-qui-aht First Nation.

MacKenzie Beach Resort
The end of MacKenzie Beach Road, 250-725-3439,
www.mackenziebeach.com

Twelve one to three-bedroom modular cabins just back from the water amongst the trees. Tenting and serviced RV sites on-site (p. 237). Indoor pool and hot tub.

Middle Beach Lodge
At the end of MacKenzie Beach Road, turn right down the private road, 866-725-2900 or 250-725-2900, www.middlebeach.com

An unparalleled location on a 16 hectare site, with two lodges and 20 cabins. A dramatic rocky headland overlooks the open ocean in front of the resort with MacKenzie Beach on the left and Middle Beach on the right. Private walking trails, artfully appointed rooms and a quiet mood make this resort a long-time favourite for Tofino getaways.

TOFINO GUIDE

HOTELS, MOTELS, AND RESORTS (NOT ON THE BEACH)

We have grouped all non-beachfront hotels, motels, resorts and lodges here. These accommodation providers are all larger facilities than vacation rentals or bed and breakfasts and are not located on the beach.

We indicate that some of the businesses are located **on the harbour**, also referred to by some as **on the inlet**.

The listings are organized, roughly, from south to north. The properties in the south end are closer to the beaches, while the properties at the north end are in the village.

Clayoquot Orca Lodge
1245 Pacific Rim Highway, 888-611-1988 or 250-725-2323, www.c-orca.com

Two separate wings make up this hotel/motel and restaurant, each with three different room sizes and configurations. The newer AnnaLise View Wing is located on the quieter, forested section of the property and the rooms here emphasize the pleasant rainforest views. The Original Wing is intended to suit travellers on a budget, providing good value for a standard hotel room with an ensuite bathroom. The friendly, resident dog indicates that many of the rooms are pet friendly.

Dolphin Motel
1190 Pacific Rim Highway, 250-725-3377, www.dolphinmotel.ca

A friendly, family run twelve-room motel located next the highway. The rooms' décor is a bit dated, but the price is right and the facilities are well kept and clean. There are communal picnic tables and BBQs around the small lawn area, but the small property is mostly parking lot and motel. Pleasant and worth the competitive price.

Weigh West Marine Resort
634 Campbell Street, 800-665-8922 or 250-725-3277, www.weighwest.com

Located on the harbour, Tofino's largest hotel/motel also has a waterfront pub and restaurant, expansive boat moorage facilities and an Adventure Centre where you can choose from fishing charters, sea kayaking tours, whale watching or hot springs tours. There are six different room types to choose from, starting at standard double rooms with no view, all the way up to self-contained waterview suites with full kitchenettes and a hot tub on the deck. Prices are competitive in all seasons but the winter specials can be impressively affordable.

Tofino Village Motel
542 Campbell Street, 250-725-2055, www.tofinomotel.com

This harbourview motel in the heart of the village has about a dozen standard double rooms and a family suite option that is larger, with a kitchenette. The friendly staff is known for their attention to cleanliness. Each room has a deck overlooking the harbour. A good option for those on a budget.

Paddler's Inn
320 Main Street, 800-863-4664 250-725-4222, www.tofinopaddlersinn.com

Operated by and located above Tofino Sea Kayaking Company (p. 96), this was Tofino's original hotel and is likely one of the town's oldest buildings. Harbour views from some of the 5 rooms, two shared bathrooms and a common kitchen and dining room.

Schooner Motel
315-321 Campbell Street, 250-725-3478, www.schoonermotel.net

A two-storey motel with ten standard, clean and welcoming hotel rooms. The larger family suites and kitchen suites have kitchenettes. The motel is located in the heart of Tofino, across from the Co-op Grocery and next door to the popular Schooner Restaurant (p. 178). Nothing fancy here, but we recommended it for folks looking for a vacancy or a relatively affordable room.

The Inn at Tough City
350 Main Street, 877-725-2021 or 250-725-2021,
www.toughcity.com

Located on the harbour, above Tough City Sushi Bar (p. 181) you will find eight small rooms, whimsically decorated with antique collectibles. During the summer season you should expect some noise from below, especially between 8 and 11 pm when the Sushi Bar is packed with slightly sloshed sushi slurpers. Expect to take home some fun and quirky stories from your encounters with the gregarious owner, Crazy Ron.

Maquinna Hotel
120 First Street, 800-665-3199 or 250-725-3261,
www.maquinnahotel.com

This three-storey hotel consists of thirty-two standard rooms with private baths. As one TripAdvisor.com reviewer points out, the hotel is "old but clean." The accommodation section of the building is located above the **Cold Beer and Wine Store** (p. 182) and **The Maquinna**, the local dance bar (p. 175), so expect some noise underneath you, especially when there is an event at the bar. We recommend that you request a room on the quieter side of the building if you choose to stay here.

Cable Cove Inn and Ashram Spa
201 Main Street, 800-663-6449 or 250-725-4236,
www.cablecoveinn.com

An adult-oriented resort with three standard rooms on the first floor, two larger rooms with vaulted ceilings on the second floor, and two suites with hot tubs on private decks. All of the rooms have gas burning fireplaces, iPod docks, and are outfitted with luxurious Indian silk. The rooms without hot tubs have indoor jacuzzi tubs in the bathrooms. On-site spa services and yoga classes are available (p. 204). High on a cliff above the Pacific, the views out to Stubbs Island and the area's original settlement of Clayoquot (p. 33) are stunning.

Duffin Cove Resort
215 Campbell Street, 888-629-2903 or 250-725-3448,
www.duffin-cove-resort.com

On the rocks high above the ocean, this resort consists of seven standard rooms, four larger suites with kitchenettes and two oceanfront cabins with expansive views. The decor is fairly dated, but the location of the property and the convenience of the suites makes this place a favourite for large families and groups looking for self-sufficiency close to town.

TOFINO GUIDE

BED AND BREAKFASTS & VACATION RENTALS

It is becoming increasingly difficult to distinguish between these two categories so we have grouped them together. Some of the properties listed here are entire home rentals, some are suites with separate entrances attached to homes, and a few are room rentals that share an entrance with a home owner. When choosing a vacation rental or bed and breakfast please do your research and make sure the accommodation is suited to your needs, by asking for specific details. Websites cannot always provide everything you might need to know.

Common misunderstandings include:

- Would you like a traditional bed and breakfast experience? Make sure to ask if breakfast is included with your stay.
- Do you require a separate entrance?
- Do you want to rent an entire house, or is an attached suite with a separate entrance ok?
- Is there a hot tub, sauna, or an outdoor shower?
- Are pets allowed and is there an extra charge for your pet?
- Are there other rental cabins or suites on the property and do these other rentals share any amenities like the hot tub or sauna?
- What type of cooking facilities are available, if any?

We have organized the following bed and breakfasts and vacation rentals into 3 different geographical areas: Near Chesterman Beach, Near MacKenzie Beach, Near Town and Tonquin Beach.

Near Cox Bay and Chesterman Beach
Abalone Inn, 1341 Pacific Rim Highway, 250-725-2386, www.tofinoinn.com

African Beach B&B, 1250 Lynn Road, 250-725-4465, www.africanbeach.com

Beach Break Lodge, 1337 Chesterman Beach Road, 877-727-3883, 250-725-3883, www.beachbreaklodge.com

Beachwood, 1368 Chesterman Beach Road, 250-725-4250, www.beachwoodtofino.com

Bird and Breakfast, 1430 Pacific Rim Highway, 250-725-2520, www.tofinobirdandbreakfast.com

Brimar B&B, 1375 Thornberg Crescent, 800-714-9373 or 250-725-3410, www.brimarbb.com

Cedars on Chesterman, Craig Road, 250-725-4280, www.cedarsonchesterman.com

Chesterman Beach B&B, 1345 Chesterman Beach Road, 250-725-3726, www.chestermanbeach.net

Chesterman House, 1293 Lynn Road, 866-393-2966, or 780-486-5415, www.chestermanhouse.com

Clayoquot Cedar House, 1398 Pacific Rim Highway, 250-725-2421, www.clayoquotassociates.com

Curious Cove, 1022 Jensen's Bay Road, 250-725-3417, www.tofinocuriouscove.com

Emerald Forest B&B, 1328 Pacific Rim Highway, 250-725-2551, www.emeraldforestretreat.com

Gold Coast Retreat, 1338 & 1340 Chesterman Beach Road, 250-725-3789, www.goldcoasttofino.com

Gull Cottage B&B, 1254 Lynn Road, 250-725-3177, www.gullcottagetofino.com

Harvey House, 1310 Lynn Road, 250-725-2364, www.harvey-house.ca

TOFINO GUIDE

Huckleberry Retreat, 1342 Chesterman Beach Road, 877-335-5331, www.islandhavens.ca

Nalu House on Chesterman, 1358 Chesterman Beach Road, 877-625-8669 or 250-725-2661, www.naluhouse.com

Pacific Coast Retreats, 1336 Chesterman Beach Road, 250-725-3990, www.pacificcoastretreats.com

Sauna House B&B, 1286 Lynn Road, 250-725-2113, www.saunahouse.net

Seafarer's B&B, 1212 Lynn Road, 250-725-1267, www.seafarersbb.com

The SeaShack, 273 Lynn Road, 604-838-7974, www.tofinoseashack.com

Seastar Beach Retreat, 1294 Lynn Road, 866-443-7827 or 250-725-2041, www.seastar-tofino.com

Tranquil Accommodations, 993 Jensen's Bay Road, 877-725-2206 or 250-725-2206, www.tranquilaccommodations.com

West Coast Accommodation, 1238 Lynn Road, 250-725-3103, www.westcoastaccommodation.com

Zoe's At North Beach, 1216 Lynn Road, 250-725-2500, www.zoesatnorthbeach.com

OVER 50 MORE VACATION RENTALS...

In addition to the vacation rental listings in this book, there are two **rental management companies** that operate over 50 properties not listed here. For more information contact:

Tofino Beach Homes, 250-725-2570,
www.tofinobeach.com

Tofino Vacation Rentals, 877-799-2779 or 250-725-2779,
www.tofinovr.com

Near MacKenzie Beach
Bird Sanctuary House & Suites, 1110 Fellowship Drive, 250-725-2741, www.tofinovacation.com

Botanical House, 1084 Pacific Rim Highway, 250-725-1220, www.tbgf.org/vacation-rental

Coastal Shoreline Place, 1108 Abraham Place, 250-725-2650, www.coastalshorelineplace.com

Cobble Wood Guesthouse & Suites, 1115 Fellowship Drive, 250-725-2741, www.tofinovacation.com

Red Crow Guesthouse, 1064 Pacific Rim Highway, 250-725-2275, www.tofinoredcrow.com

Summerhill Guest House, 1101 Fellowship Drive, 250-725-2447, www.tofinolodging.com

Tigh-na Clayoquot Cottage, 1040 Campbell Street, 250-725-4490, www.tofino-holidays.com

Tofino Hideaway, 664 Parlee Place, 250-652 2669, www.tofinohideaway.com

TOFINO GUIDE

Near Town and Tonquin Beach
Adventure Tofino B&B, 615 Pfeiffer Crescent, 250-725-2895, www.adventuretofino.com

Cannery Retreat, 230 Main Street, 888-492-6662, www.canneryretreat.com

Clayoquot Retreat B&B, 120 Arnet Road, 250-725-3305, www.clayoquotretreat.com

High Tide, 151 Eik Road, 877-335-5331, www.islandhavens.ca

Meares Retreat B&B, 140 Arnet Road, 250-725-4234, www.mearesretreat.com

Ocean Dream Vacation Home, 800 Campbell Street, 250-725-4282, www.oceandream.ca

On The Beach B&B, 351 Tonquin Park Road, 250-704-0207, www.tofino-onthebeach.com

Ospray Lodge B&B, 450 Neill Street, 800-221-1140 or 250-725-2669, www.tofinolodge.com

Storm Bay B&B, 680 Campbell Street, 250-725-3492, www.stormbay.ca

Strawberry Isle Retreat, Strawberry Island, 250-725-8658

Tides Inn B&B, 160 Arnet Road, 250-725-3765, www.tidesinntofino.com

Tofino Inlet Cottages, 350 Olsen Road, 866-725-3441 or 250-725-441, www.tofinoinletcottages.com

What to do if you see a...
DUNGENESS CRAB

Try to imagine this creature's kinky sex life. Males are attracted by pheromones in the urine of female Dungeness crabs (*Metacarcinus magister*). Once he finds a likely mate, the male initiates a pre-mating embrace that lasts for several days. He tucks the female under him, so their abdomens touch and their heads face each other. Eventually the female urinates on or near the antennae of the male indicating her readiness to mate. Before mating, she molts, losing her shell. Complicated enough?

TOFINO GUIDE

HOSTELS

These low cost accommodation providers offer several types of lodging that centre around a central, shared kitchen and lounge area. Each facility has the option for shared or private rooms as well as shared or private bathrooms. All of the accommodation options include bedding. Reservations are absolutely necessary in the summer season.

Whalers on the Point Guesthouse, 81 West Street, 250-725-3443, www.tofinohostel.com

Clayoquot Field Station, 1084 Pacific Rim Highway, 250-725-1220, www.tbgf.org

Tofino Trek Inn, 231 Main Street, 250-725-2791, www.tofinotrekinn.com

ACCOMMODATION AT HOT SPRINGS COVE

Hot Springs Lodge, 250-670-1106
A basic six-room waterfront hotel located in Hot Springs Cove village, the Hesquiaht First Nation community across the harbour from the hot springs trailhead.

The InnChanter (floating) Bed & Breakfast,
250-670-1149 or 250-670-1156, www.innchanter.com
Moored at the dock adjacent to the hot springs trailhead. Five staterooms, a common room with wood burning fireplace, a small library, and an onboard chef to prepare and serve the included meals.

Maquinna Campground, 250-670-1106
This is a private campground owned and operated by the Hesquiaht First Nation. It is located at the hot springs trailhead. Bring your own tent and rent a site for $20 per night per tent. The campground fees are collected by an attendant, usually after the tent has been set up. Toilet facilities are on-site.

CAMPGROUNDS

Please note that camping outside of a designated campground in Tofino is illegal. It is also rude. Bylaw officers in Tofino are on the job, consistently **enforcing bylaws that prohibit illegal camping**. Please respect our neighbours and **make a reservation with a campground well in advance** if you plan on camping.

Bella Pacifica Campground
400 MacKenzie Beach Road, 250-725-3400,
www.bellapacifica.com
Over 150 RV and tent sites on MacKenzie Beach

Crystal Cove Beach Resort
1165 Cedarwood Place, 250-725-4213,
www.crystalcovebeachresort.com
72 RV and tent sites on MacKenzie Beach

Campground at Long Beach Golf Course
1850 Pacific Rim Highway, 250-725-3332,
www.longbeachgolfcourse.com
76 RV and tent sites close to Long Beach

Green Point Campground
Pacific Rim National Park, 877-737-3783 (reservations phone), 250-726-3500 (park information phone), www.pccamping.ca
Over 90 RV and tent sites on Long Beach

MacKenzie Beach Campground
End of MacKenzie Beach Road, 250-725-3439,
www.mackenziebeach.com
Over 60 RV and tent sites on MacKenzie Beach

TOFINO GUIDE

GLAMPING: GLAMOROUS CAMPING

Do you crave a wilderness experience but cannot live without a goose down duvet and 5-star meals? Glamping has you covered. The **Clayoquot Wilderness Resort**, located about 45 minutes from Tofino by boat or 10 minutes by air, is one of the innovators in this hybrid experience. The resort provides all-inclusive packages to guests who sleep in deluxe prospector-style canvas tents. The tents are outfitted with electrical outlets and many of the luxuries that you would expect in an upscale resort: puffy beds, plush reading chairs and sofas, terry cotton robes, high-end skin care products. There are even two Lounge Tents, one equipped with a billiard table and one with a computer ready for internet access. The world-class food is cooked for you by the resident chef and his team in an expansive open-air kitchen. A few of the activities that will keep you busy at the resort in between your comfortable sleeps: rock climbing, horseback riding, fishing charters, massage, yoga, clay shooting and cooking classes.

Clayoquot Wilderness Resort, 888-333-5405 or 250-726-8235, www.wildretreat.com

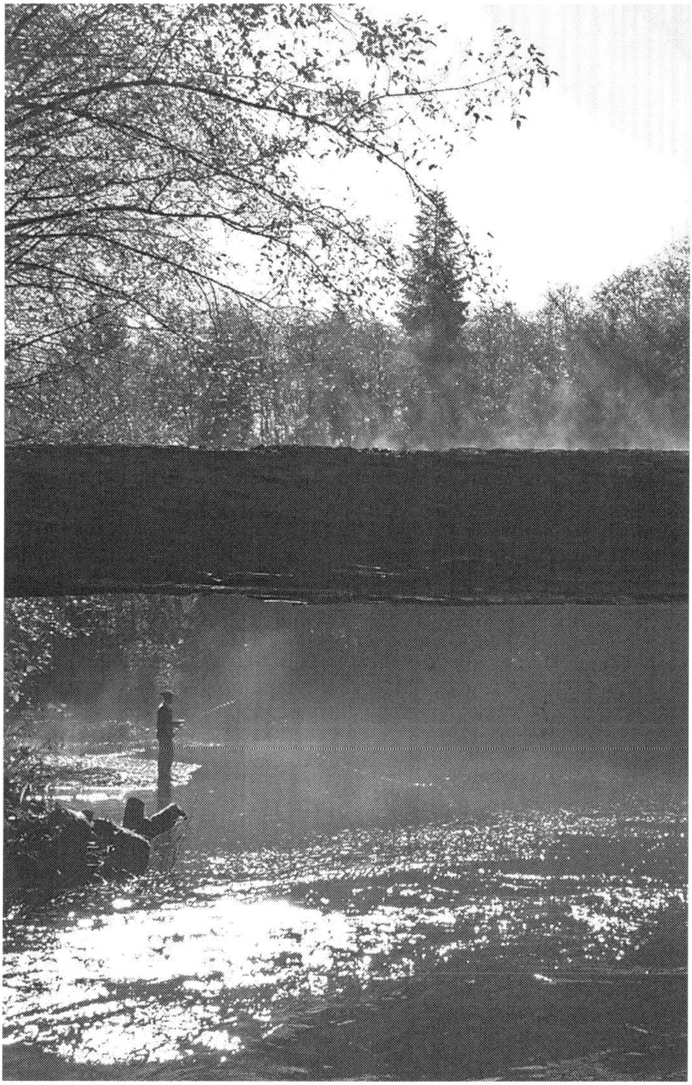

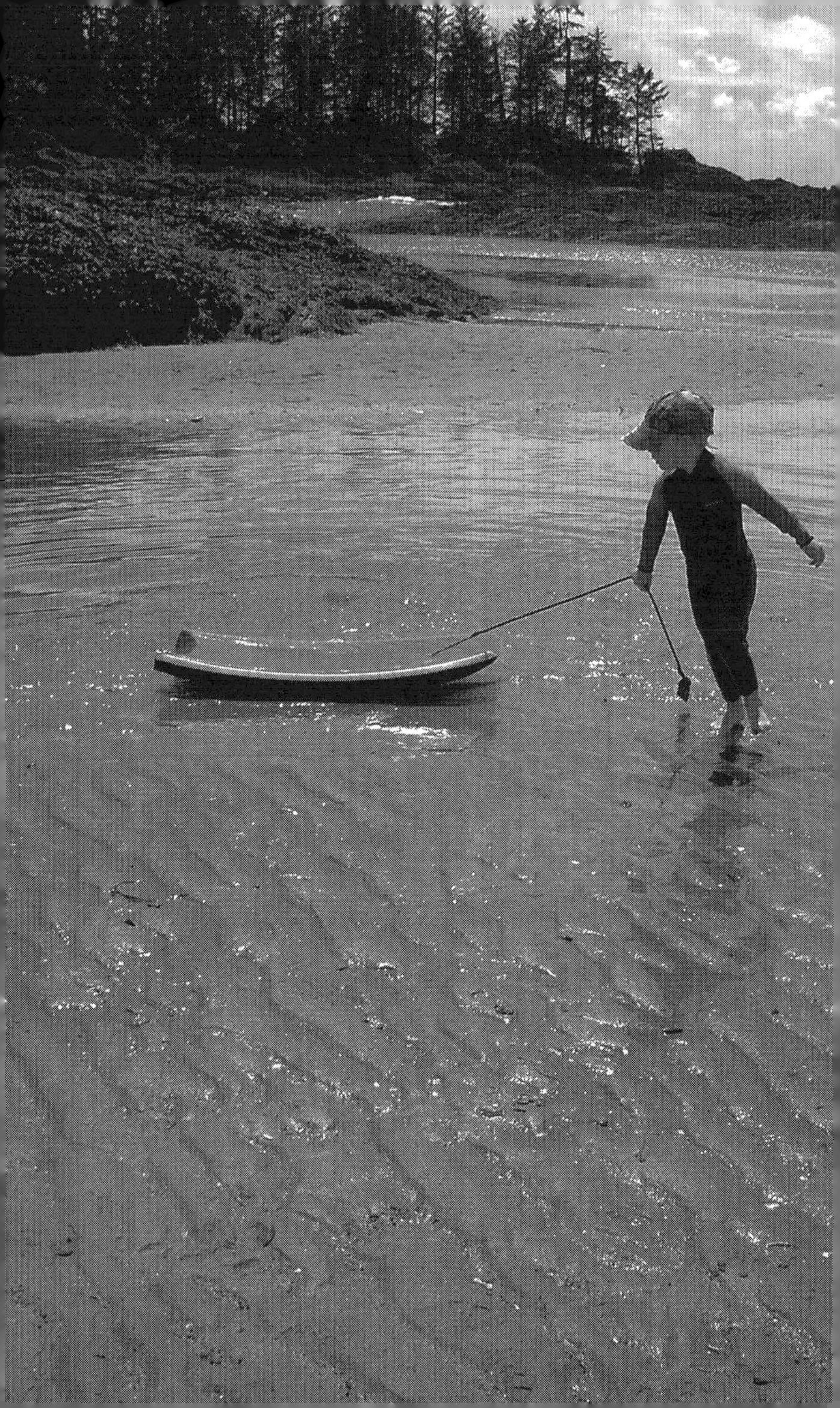

LOCAL TRANSPORTATION

Tofino Transit

The Beach Bus

Taxi

Water Taxis

Boat Launches

TOFINO GUIDE

TOFINO TRANSIT

346 Campbell Street, 866-986-3466 or 250-725-2871, www.tofinobus.com
Exceptional local transportation is operated by the crew at Tofino Bus during July and August. The 14-passenger vans pick up and drop off passengers and their surfboards at a variety of marked stops between downtown Tofino, the resorts, and the beaches. Check the times on the marked stops, or at www.tofinobus.com, or pick up a schedule at any of the three Visitor Centres (p. 25). $2 one-way gets you anywhere between Cox Bay and the Tofino Bus station, near First and Campbell Street.

THE BEACH BUS

346 Campbell Street, 866-986-3466 or 250-725-2871, www.tofinobus.com
Operates three scheduled trips between Tofino and Ucluelet with stops in between. $10 one way or $15 return gets you as far as Long Beach. $15 one way or $21 return gets you to Ucluelet. Multi-day passes are available. Check the schedule at www.tofinobus.com or pick up a schedule at any of the three Visitor Centres.

TAXI

Tofino Taxi, 250-725-3333, Call for pick-up

WATER TAXIS

"Water taxi" in our area is a loosely defined term, basically meaning any marine vessel that will get you where you want to go for a set price. If a company does not have an office address listed below, then give the company a call or head down to **First Street Dock** (p. 116) and ask around. Payments are almost always in cash. You should try to have small bills in order to provide exact change. The cost depends on how far you are going, but will start around $25 for a short local trip and go up from there. Tipping the driver is not routine on water taxis but drivers are never offended by gratuities.

Ahousaht Pride Water Taxi, 250-670-9563, First Street Dock
Regular service between Marktosis (Ahousaht) on Flores Island and Tofino
Departs twice daily from Tofino at 10:30 am and 4:00 pm
Departs twice daily from Marktosis at 8:30 am and 1:00 pm

Clayoquot Connections, 250 726-8789
Regular service: offers many different tours and drop offs. Cash only.

The Matlahaw, 250-670-1106, First Street Dock
Service to Hot Spring Cove operated by the Hesquiaht First Nation. Cash only.

Ocean Outfitters Water Taxi, 368 Main Street, 877-906-2326 or 250-725-2866, www.oceanoutfitters.bc.ca
Regular service to the Big Tree Trail and offers many different tours and drop offs. Accepts Visa and MasterCard.

Tofino Water Taxi, 877-726-5485, www.tofinowatertaxi.com
Regular service to the Big Tree Trail and offers many different tours and drop offs. Accepts Visa and MasterCard.

John Tom, 250-725-3747, First Street Dock
Often available for a range of drop offs. Cash only.

BOAT LAUNCHES

Fourth Street Dock Boat Launch
Tofino Harbour Authority, 250-725-4441

Motor boats can be launched for a $10 fee from the **Fourth Street Dock** at the bottom of Fourth Street. Parking for your vehicle and trailer at the dock after you launch is possible ($5/day for vehicle, additional $5/day for trailer), but parking areas here are limited, especially during the summer, so arrive early if you need to park at the dock. Pay the Harbour Master for the launch and parking at the small cedar building at the top of the dock.

If there is no parking at the dock, drive three blocks back up Fourth Street to Gibson Street and find street parking near the Wickaninnish Elementary School or a block further up on Fourth Street adjacent to the school's baseball field. It is legal to park a vehicle with a trailer on the street, as long as the trailer is attached to the vehicle.

Grice Bay Boat Launch

Grice Bay is on the Tofino Inlet side of Esowista Peninsula. This area was a favourite feeding ground for resident grey whales in past years during the summer months, but sightings have not been as common recently.

From here, a public boat launch provides great access to the north and east sides of Meares Island and to Tofino Inlet. Please note that **four-wheel drive is recommended** if you are planning on launching or retrieving your boat here at a low tide.

Parking is usually available in the large parking area at the boat launch. **A Park Pass is required to park your vehicle here.** Purchase your Park Pass at another location before you arrive if you plan on parking here. See page 76 for more information and a list of purchasing locations.

The road down to Grice Bay is pleasant, winding through some remarkable trees and ending with an excellent view of the eastern end of Meares Island. The trout fishing is quite good here on a high, slack tide during April and May.

Directions
Turn left on Grice Road at the Golf Course/Campground sign about 14 km south of the Post Office on the highway. Stay to your left until you reach the inlet side of the ocean at the end of the road. Drive cautiously on this narrow, paved road. There are hidden bumpy sections that can be very alarming, especially if you are towing a boat.

Small Craft Boat Launching
Kayaks and canoes can be launched from an excellent public kayak launch located beside First Street Dock, in front of the Fred Tibbs condo building at the end of First Street. **Motorized boat launch is prohibited from all public beaches, so do not even think about launching your jet ski on Chesterman or any other beach**. Infractions carry fines as well as an environmental penalty.

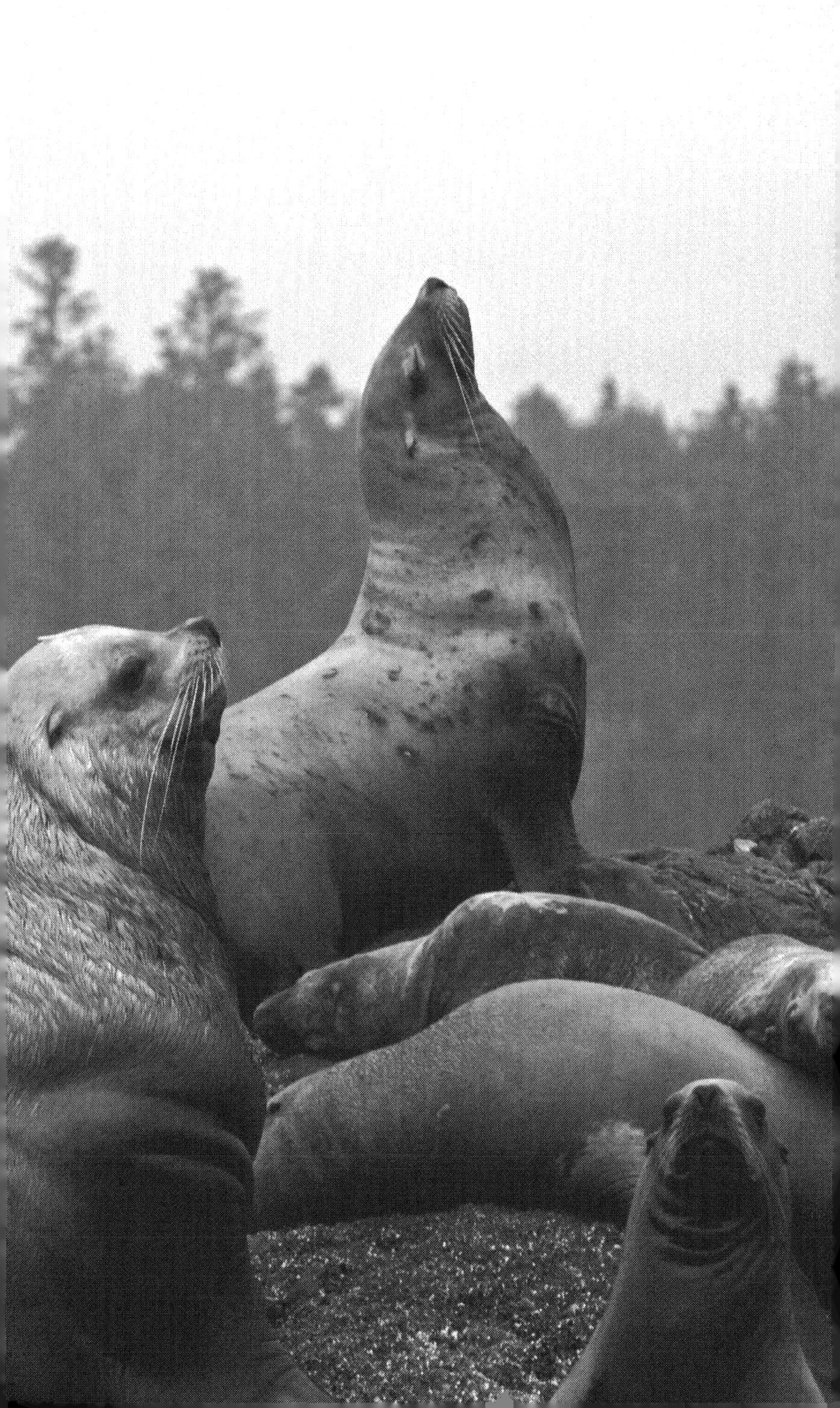

SERVICES

Banking, Foreign Currency Exchange, and ATMs (Cash Machines)

Fuel Service

Laundry & Showers

Pharmacy

Library, Museums, Societies

Churches

Recycling

Tofino Radio

Periodicals

Post Office

TOFINO GUIDE

BANKING, FOREIGN CURRENCY EXCHANGE, AND ATMS (CASH MACHINES)

CIBC Tofino Branch, 301 Campbell Street, 250-725-3321
Open Monday - Thursday, 9:30 am to 4 pm; Friday, 9:30 am to 5 pm
Cash machine on-site (24 hours)
Limited currency exchange available. US Dollars are exchanged regularly, but it is best to phone ahead if you need to exchange currency. The branch will try to accommodate your request.

Coastal Community Credit Union, 390 Main Street, 250-725-2366
Open Tuesday – Saturday 10 am to 3 pm
Cash machine on-site (24 hours)
Currency exchange for credit union members only.

Tofino Pharmacy, 360 Campbell Street, 250-725-3101
Currency exchange service is available at the pharmacy counter in the back of the store. US dollars and Euros are exchanged regularly and other currencies *may* be exchanged. Please phone or inquire in person about foreign currency exchange.
Pharmacy counter hours: Monday-Friday, 10:30 am – 5:30 pm; Saturday, 11 am – 5 pm; Sunday 11 am – 12 pm and 4 pm – 5 pm
Cash machine on-site

Other cash machines (ATMs) are located inside the following: Co-op Gas Station, Co-op Grocery, LA Grocery, Long Beach Market (Gas N Go)

FUEL SERVICE

Co-op Gas Bar
797 Campbell Street, 250-725-3225
Regular/unleaded + the only diesel stop in town. RV Dump Station. Coin operated vehicle cleaning vacuum. Free compressed air.

Gas 'N Go / Long Beach Market
921 Campbell Street, 250-725-2050
Gasoline and propane. Gas station snacks, milk and a few other basic food supplies, firewood and some camping supplies.

Method Marine (known locally as Whitey's)
380 Main Street on the Pier, 250-725-3251
Between First and Fourth Street docks if travelling by boat
Marine fuel, propane, fishing tackle and marine supplies

LAUNDRY & SHOWERS

Long Beach Laundromat
Located on Fourth Street (next to Tuff Beans)
Only coin-operated laundry in town. Very busy in the summer. Please don't ask nearby businesses for change. Two coin-operated showers – bring lots of loonies and quarters as the change machine may not be working.

MacKenzie Beach Resort and Ocean Village Beach Resort have showers at their swimming pool facilities (**Indoor Swimming**, p. 213).

PHARMACY

Tofino Pharmacy
360 Campbell Street, 250-725-3101
Prescription drugs, sundries, souvenirs, postcards, boogie board sales and rentals, Internet-enabled computers for hire. The store is open 7 days a week 9:30 am to 9:00 pm in the summer (shorter hours 7 days a week the rest of the year). The pharmacy is open to fill prescriptions 10:30 am - 5:30 pm Monday – Friday and 11:00 am – 5:00 pm on Saturday.

LIBRARY, MUSEUMS, SOCIETIES

Tofino Public Library (a branch of Vancouver Island Regional Library)
331 Main Street (Under the Tofino Legion), 250-725-3713, www.virl.bc.ca
Open: Wed, Thurs, Fri 3 – 7 pm; Sat 10 – 12 and 1 – 5 pm
An excellent small library with a particularly good selection of local reading material, magazines and children's books.
Internet-enabled computers, but there are only two terminals and it is busy in the peak season.

Clayoquot Community Theatre, 121 Third Street (accessed from Campbell St)
Event schedule varies. Check local listings for films, plays, lectures and concerts. Watch for the sign out front that will read Event Tonight. Monday Night Movie series is good if you like artsy-enviro documentaries and independent feature films. Check www. tofinomovies.blogspot.com for the schedule and a write-up of the current month's films.

Maritime Museum
564 Campbell Street (in an older shed in the lower parking lot), 250-725-3256
Located in a resident's old garage, the Maritime Museum displays treasures that have been salvaged from the area's many wrecks. Remember that story of the *Tonquin* (p. 62)? The anchor is usually housed here. The museum relies on volunteers to tend the collections and host visitors, so hours are not consistent. If you are interested in visiting, call ahead.

Raincoast Education Society
1084 Pacific Rim Highway (in the Tofino Botanical Gardens), 250-725-2560, www.raincoasteducation.org

The society operates the **Raincoast Interpretive Centre**, an interactive environment to study issues related to the rainforest. They arrange and provide scheduled lectures, fieldtrips and other natural and cultural history programs. Open most weekdays with daily hours during the summer months.

Tonquin Foundation, 250-725-4488,
www.tonquinfoundation.org
A local, non-profit society "dedicated to the exploration, preservation and interpretation of the rich and diverse maritime heritage of North America's Westcoast."

What to do if you see a...

DUCK

Stay calm. Slowly crouch down to the same eye level as the duck **without making eye contact**. If you have any bread products, surrender them at once, breaking them into small pieces that can be gently tossed toward the aggressor. Do not make any fast movements. After the duck has eaten the bread, she will lose interest in you and it will be safe to leave the area. Be careful as Mallards (*Anas platyrhynchos* -- a common but easily agitated species of waterfowl in Clayoquot Sound) often travel in intimidating pairs.

CHURCHES

The pastors and ministers at the two churches in Tofino alternate their schedules with Ucluelet churches. This creates some scheduling irregularities. If you need more information about church schedules, please call the phone numbers listed below.

St. Columba Church, 110 Second Street, 250-726-7318
Anglican and United Church of Canada
Sunday Service at 11 am
Minister on-site Wednesdays

St. Francis of Assisi Church, 411 Main Street, 250-725-3224
Roman Catholic
Mass Saturdays at 5 pm
There is usually Mass Tuesdays and Thursdays at 5 pm

Tofino Bible Fellowship
Regular Sunday gathering – Call for details: 250-725-4289

RECYCLING

Recycling schemes in Tofino are constantly changing and improving. Ask at your hotel, bed and breakfast or campsite for details.

Bottle Depot
671 Industrial Way
Open Monday, Wednesday, Friday, Saturday 10 am – 3:30 pm.
Provides refunds for returns of most beverage containers

TOFINO RADIO

91.5 FM for **CBC National Public Radio** (CBC One). Hourly news, talk shows and music

90.1 FM for **CHMZ Long Beach Radio**. "Tofino Radio Serving the Real West Coast." Local news, weather, surf reports, and a variety of pop and rock music. Broadcast from the end of First Street Dock.

104.7 FM for a rebroadcast of **CFMI 101 Classic Rock** from Vancouver

1260 am for **Parks Canada information** and weather

PERIODICALS

Ha-Shilth-Sa, www.nuuchahnulth.org/tribal-council/hashilth.html

Canada's oldest First Nations' newspaper is published by the Nuu-chah-nulth Tribal Council. The paper is difficult to find in Tofino, but is freely available online.

Tofino Time, www.tofinotime.com
A free monthly magazine with articles and advertisements geared to visitor activities. Check out the excellent monthly calendar of events at the back. Great maps too.

The Westcoaster, www.westcoaster.ca
A good online source for regional and local news and gossip.

Westerly News, www.westerlynews.ca
1701 Peninsula Road, Ucluelet: 250-726-7029
The weekly newspaper for Tofino, Ucluelet and surrounding First Nations communities is available at all convenience and grocery stores for about $1, or freely available online. The Letters to the Editor section is often more entertaining than TV. Good classifieds for long term and seasonal accommodation.

POST OFFICE

The Post Office, **Canada Post**, is located at First and Campbell Streets at the only traffic light in town.
Hours: 8:30-5:30 Mon-Fri, Saturday 9:00-1:00

RECOMMENDED READING

Tofino has more writers per capita than San Francisco in the 1950s. Many of the following books are written by local or regional authors. To find any of the following titles, phone **Mermaid Tales** *(250-725-2125, www.mermaidbooks.ca) or* **Wildside Books** *(250-725-4222, www.tofino-kayaking.com). If the title is not available there, try the library, Amazon.com or AbeBooks.com.*

TOFINO GUIDE

Cultural History and Contemporary Perspectives

Vancouver Island's West Coast 1762-1962; George Nicholson; 1962

Clayoquot Soundings: A History of Clayoquot Sound, 1880s - 1980s; Walter Guppy; 1997

Cougar Annie's Garden; Margaret Horsfield; 1999

Since the Time of the Transformers: The Ancient Heritage of the Nuu-Chah-Nulth, Ditidaht, and Makah; Alan D. McMillan; 2000

The Tofino Kid: From India to This Wild West Coast; Anthony Guppy; 2000

The Cedar Surf: An Informal History of Surfing in British Columbia; Grant Shilling; 2003

Living on the Edge: Nuu-Chah-Nulth History from an Ahousaht Chief's Perspective; Earl Maquinna George; 2003

Tales from the West Coast: Smugglers, Sea Monsters, and Other Stories; Adrienne Mason; 2003

West Coast Adventures: Shipwrecks, Lighthouses, and Rescues Along Canada's West Coast; Adrienne Mason; 2003

Chasing Clayoquot: A Wilderness Almanac; David Pitt-Brooke; 2004

Silent Inlet; Joanna Streetly; 2005

Tsawalk: A Nuu-chah-nulth Worldview; E. Richard Atleo; 2005

Journeys; Frank Harper; 2006

Tonquin: The Ghost Ship of Clayoquot Sound; David W. Griffiths; 2007

Builders of the Pacific Coast; Lloyd Kahn; 2008

Voices from the Sound: Chronicles of Clayoquot Sound and Tofino, 1899-1929; Margaret Horsfield; 2008

Encyclopedia of Raincoast Place Names, Andrew Scott; 2009

Road's End: Tales of Tofino; Shirley Langer; 2009

Natural History
Tofino Botanical Gardens Field Guide; George Patterson (ed.)

The New Savory Wild Mushroom; Margaret McKenny and Daniel E. Stuntz; 1987

All That the Rain Promises and More: A Hip Pocket Guide to Western Mushrooms; David Arora; 1991

Coastal Temperate Rain Forests: Ecological Characteristics, Status and Distribution Worldwide; Ecotrust and Conservation International; 1992 (www.ecotrust.org/publications/ctrf.html)

Plants of Coastal British Columbia Including Washington Oregon and Alaska; Jim Pojar and Andy MacKinnon; 1994

Mammals of British Columbia; Tamara Eder; 2001

Whales and other Marine Mammals of British Columbia and Alaska; Tamara Eder; 2001

Adventure Guides
The Wild Coast 1: A Kayaking, Hiking and Recreational Guide for North and West Vancouver Island; John Kimantas; 2005

Coastal Hikes: A Guide to West Coast Hiking in British Columbia and Washington State; Philip Stone; 2007

Ahousaht Wild Side Heritage Trail Guidebook; Stanley Sam Jr.; 1997

Wild Side Guide to Vancouver Island's Pacific Rim; Jaqueline Windh; 2006

TOFINO GUIDE

Children's Material
Westcoast Activity Book; Westcoast Vancouver Island Aquatic Management Board; 2006

The Oyster Who Looked at the Sky; Darcy Dobell and Marion Syme; 2008

WILD about the West Coast Discovery Book; Adrienne Mason and Marion Syme; 2009

Canadian Hydrographic Service Nautical Charts
#3673 Clayoquot Sound, Tofino Inlet- Millar Channel; 1:40,000

#3674 Clayoquot Sound, Millar Channel-Estevan Pt.; 1:40,000

#3685 Tofino; 1:20,000

What to do if you see a...

MISTAKE!!

You mean we goofed? Did that hiking trail turn left instead of right? Or perhaps you'd just like to share something new, or a kind word of advice to fellow travellers?

Contact Tofino Guide

We welcome your comments, corrections and suggestions.

Please send all correspondence by email or by mail to the ***Tofino Guide*** address:

Tofino Guide

c/o Tofino Internet Services Ltd.

PO Box 83
Tofino, BC V0R 2Z0
Canada

Email: tofino.guide@gmail.com
Web: www.tofino-bc.com

ACKNOWLEDGEMENTS

Thank you to my partners in exploration and adventure: my wife, Sarah, and my children, Reed and Chloe.

Thanks also to Margaret Horsfield, who edited the manuscript, and to my dad, Peter Platenius, for his eagle-eyed assistance.

Made in the USA
Charleston, SC
14 April 2011